FISH & SHELLFISH

Charlotte Walker

ANOTHER BEST-SELLING VOLUME FROM HPBooks®

Publisher: Rick Bailey; Editorial Director: Retha M. Davis
Editor: Carroll Latham; Art Director: Don Burton
Typography: Cindy Coatsworth, Michelle Claridge
Line Drawings: Paul Fitzgerald, Pam Peterson
Book Design: Paul Fitzgerald
Food Stylist: Carol Flood Peterson; Photography: George de Gennaro Studios

The author wishes to thank Barbara Fleming, Betty Miller,
Ann Ny Pang, Patti Litman, Virginia Ladensohn and husband, Steve Pisinski,
for their untiring support and help.

Special thanks are given to Grainware, Inc., Edward Parmacek, President, for loan of photographic props.

Published by HPBooks®
P.O. Box 5367, Tucson, AZ 85703   602/888-2150
ISBN 0-89586-258-1
Library of Congress Catalog Card Number 84-80775
©1984 Fisher Publishing, Inc. Printed in the U.S.A.
Cover Photo: Bouillabaisse, page 104.

CONTENTS

Charlotte Walker

Charlotte Walker enjoys developing recipes and trying out her ideas on husband, Steve. In addition to a busy work schedule, Charlotte enjoys entertaining. Fish and shellfish are the perfect main dish when entertaining. She has updated some of the classic fish dishes with new and exciting flavor additions. Fish dishes don't have to be dull or bland. Prove it to yourself by using some of Charlotte's delicate, savory and piquant sauces.

As an advocate of time-saving, she finds that fish is the ultimate fast-food. Fish is light, nutritious and delicious, as well as fast to prepare.

Charlotte is an instructor at a professional culinary school in San Francisco, a successful home economist, writer and food stylist. She has contributed articles to several food magazines. She also creates and implements food-related special events for clients. Charlotte sits on the boards of the San Francisco Professional Food Society and San Francisco Home Economists in Business, and is a member of the American Institute of Wine & Food and International Association of Cooking Schools.

Charlotte has traveled extensively in Mexico, Europe and the Orient, and has participated in culinary-study trips to Mexico, Italy and Hong Kong. She and her husband live in San Francisco.

Basics About Fish & Shellfish

We're eating more fish and shellfish today than ever before as refrigerated airplanes and trucks ship fresh seafood around the world. If you serve fish tonight, it may be from New Zealand, Norway, Mexico, Maine, California or Alaska.

Fish and shellfish fit today's trend toward lighter, more nutritious easy-to-prepare foods. They are excellent sources of high-quality protein, vitamins and minerals. Fish are low in saturated fats and sodium, and—pound for pound—have fewer calories than red meat.

Fish and shellfish are gaining popularity because of the speed with which they cook. They are *fast-food* in the best sense—a perfect choice for busy people.

Fish are available in a variety of sizes and shapes—from tiny to over 50 feet long, and from a fraction of an ounce to several thousand pounds. Most commercial species come under two broad categories, *roundfish* and *flatfish,* page 8. The majority of fish are round-bodied with the eyes on the sides of the head. They have long, slender bodies. Flatfish include flounder, sole, turbot and halibut. They are platter-shape with eyes facing upward, and have a dark upper skin and white belly. They swim horizontally along the sea bottom.

Some species of fish have unfamiliar and strange-sounding names, such as porgy, sheepshead and tilefish. Others are called by more than one name. For example, angler may be sold as monkfish, goosefish or lotte—all the same fish.

Don't let the bewildering names intimidate you. By comparing fish you know with less familiar varieties, you can make substitutions easily. There's really no mystery to cooking fish.

When buying fish, be flexible. Rather than looking for a particular fish, go to the market with a cooking technique or recipe in mind. Depending on weather and season, catches of fish vary considerably. You may find that your retailer doesn't have cod, but has lingcod—a good substitute for cod.

If you're unfamiliar with the fish that's available, ask the retailer about its fat content. Fat content largely determines the flavor, color, texture and cooking method of any fish.

Confused? Don't be. Once you learn to cook by technique, you can cook any fish that fits that technique.

Fish are divided into three categories: low-fat or lean, moderate-fat, and high-fat. The oil of lean fish is concentrated in the liver—hence the name, cod-liver oil. Lean fish have a mild flavor and white or light color. The oil is distributed throughout the flesh of moderate-fat and high-fat fish, giving a more pronounced flavor, a firm and sometimes meat-like texture and a darker color.

Most fish are lean or low-fat. Lean fish have an average of 2 percent fat and include angler, cod, scrod, drum, sole, flounder, haddock, halibut, red snapper, catfish, perch and whiting. Moderate-fat fish contain an average of 6 percent fat and include trout, pompano, mahi mahi and some varieties of salmon. High-fat fish, such as sturgeon, herring, mackerel, tuna, bluefish, shad and some varieties of salmon, contain about 12 percent fat.

Cook lean fish by using methods that retain or add moisture or fat, such as poaching, steaming, sautéing, deep-frying, baking in sauces and simmering in soups and stews. Moderate-fat fish adapt to almost any method. High-fat fish are excellent broiled, grilled or baked at a high temperature.

Never overcook fish. It is naturally tender and should be cooked only until the flesh turns opaque and is firm. Overcooked fish shrinks, toughens and is dry.

There are three methods for testing doneness of fish. The Canadian Department of Fisheries suggests measuring fish at the thickest part and allowing 10 minutes cooking time for every inch of thickness when the fish is fresh and 20 minutes for every inch when frozen. However, fish sometimes overcooks with this method.

Many older cookbooks recommend cooking fish until it flakes when tested with a fork. Flaking means the flesh breaks apart. However, fish continues to cook after it is removed from the heat. If cooked to the point of flaking, it may be overdone by the time it is eaten.

The best test for doneness is to cook the fish until it turns from transparent to opaque. Check the fish by cutting into the center of the thickest portion. When the flesh becomes slightly opaque, remove it from the heat. Opacity is a reliable test for doneness of shellfish. You can also test a large whole fish with a rapid-response thermometer—fish is done at 140F (60C).

This book is organized by cooking techniques: poaching, steaming and steeping; baking and microwaving; sautéing, pan-frying and deep-frying; and broiling and grilling. Once you learn to cook by technique, you can cook any fish, regardless of species or size. Discussions of cooking techniques are presented in chapter introductions.

Purchasing Fish & Shellfish

Fish and shellfish are extremely perishable. From the moment fish leave the water, bacteria and natural enzymes begin to break down the flesh. Cold temperatures slow deterioration, but even under the best conditions, seafood should be eaten as soon as possible after it's caught. Because of its short storage time, many fish are gutted or filleted and frozen aboard fishing boats.

Purchase fish the day you plan to eat it. Whole fish are generally the best buy. When you cut up the fish yourself, you can use the bones and trimmings to make fish stock—the basis of many soups and stews. It is easier to judge quality when the fish are whole. Use the guidelines below when purchasing fish and shellfish.

Purchasing & Handling Frozen Fish—Frozen fish provide variety year-round and, in many parts of the world, are the most available form of fish. When purchasing frozen fish, select undamaged, solidly frozen packages without discoloration, signs of drying or fishy aroma. Take seafood as quickly as possible from the store to your home—no side trips! Leave frozen seafood in its original wrapping and place it in the freezer immediately.

Thawing causes the delicate flesh of fish and shellfish to break down and lose moisture. Therefore, cook fish before it is thawed completely. An exception is fish and shellfish that require breading, deep-frying or stuffing. Generally, cook frozen fish about twice as long as fresh fish or until it tests done. For ice-glazed or ice-packed whole fish, page 9, thaw long enough to remove the outer coating of ice. Thaw fillets and steaks until they can be separated or cut into serving pieces.

Judging Freshness

Fresh Whole Fish
- Eyes should be bright, clear and full. As fish age, the eyes become cloudy and sunken. An exception to this is deep-water fish that are brought up quickly from the ocean bottom, causing severe pressure in, and damage to, the eyes.
- Gills are bright pink or red when fresh. Lift up the gill cover and remove any mud from the gills to see the color. Gills become gray, brownish or dark green and slimy with age.
- Flesh will be firm and elastic so it springs back when you press it with your finger.
- Skin should be shiny and bright-colored, and the scales tightly attached.
- Aroma will be fresh, mild and faintly marine if it is an ocean fish. With age, a strong *fishy* aroma develops.

Fillets & Steaks
- Fillets and steaks should have a fresh-cut, moist appearance, firm texture and fresh odor. There should be no trace of drying, or yellow or brown discoloration.

Frozen Fish
- Frozen fish should be solidly frozen and covered with an undamaged tightly fitting, moisture- and vapor-proof wrap. There should be no cottony white or dark spots, icy edges or signs of drying and deterioration.

Common Market Forms: 1. Whole fish: Eastern Perch (Scup); 2. Dressed fish: Trout; 3. Pan-dressed fish: Trout; 4. Steaks: Salmon; 5. Fillets: Catfish.

Common Market Forms

- **Whole fish** are sold as they come from the water. They must be dressed before cooking.
- **Dressed fish** have internal organs—*viscera*—and gills removed. Head, fins, tail and scales are usually intact. Some retailers consider dressed fish to have the head removed.
- **Pan-dressed fish** have the scales, viscera, gills and head removed. Fins and tail may or may not be trimmed or removed.
- **Chunks** are cross-sections of fish, 4 to 6 inches thick. They include skin and bones.
- **Steaks** are crosswise slices, 1/4 to 1-1/2 inches thick. They include skin and bones. Salmon, halibut, swordfish and other large fish are commonly sold as steaks.
- **Fillets** are boneless sides of flesh cut from the backbone and ribs. They generally range in weight from 2 to 12 ounces, and may be skinned or have the skin on. Fillets are the most common form of fish available, fresh or frozen.
- **Scallops,** not to be confused with the mollusk, page 28, are thin slices cut from thick fish fillets, such as salmon or lingcod.
- **Frozen portions** and **fish sticks** are available in uniform, ready-to-cook pieces. They are sold raw, pre-cooked, breaded or dipped in batter.
- **Salt cod** is sold in fillets or pieces cut from fillets, and is often available in one-pound weights, packaged in wooden boxes. The amount of salt used to cure the cod varies, depending on the curing method and weather conditions. Heavily salted cod, which is hard as a board, must be soaked 24 hours to freshen it. Less salty, more tender cod may need to be soaked only 12 hours.
- **Finnan haddie** is uncooked, cold-smoked haddock fillets. It was first popularized in the Scottish seaport of Findhorn. *Haddie* is Scottish for haddock. The best finnan haddie is golden and moist with a delicate oak-smoke flavor. True finnan haddie is recognized by its small size and intact backbone.

Thaw all frozen fish and shellfish in the refrigerator. To thaw fish more quickly, leave it in the original wrapper. Place it in a plastic bag, then submerge the bag in a pan of cold water. Or, thaw fish in a microwave oven following the manufacturer's instructions. Cook or refrigerate fish as soon as it is thawed. Do not re-freeze thawed fish or shellfish.

Storing Fish—Wrap fresh fish in plastic wrap or foil, then store it in the coldest part of the refrigerator. Cook fish within 24 hours of purchase.

Keep smoked or marinated fish products refrigerated. Serve within two or three days of purchase. Dried and salted fish, such as salt cod, can be stored at room temperature in a dry place up to six months.

Freezing Fish—If you're faced with an abundance of fresh fish, freezing is your best option. Gut the fish immediately, then freeze it within 24 hours. In the meantime, keep it iced or refrigerated.

High-fat fish, such as sablefish, tuna, sturgeon and salmon, will keep fresh longer if treated with an ascorbic-acid mixture. Prepare a solution of 2 tablespoons ascorbic acid—available at drug stores—to 1 quart cold water. Dip fish in this solution for 30 seconds. Lean and moderate-fat fish, such as sole, flounder, halibut and turbot, keep best when dipped 30 seconds in a brine made of 1/2 cup salt to 1 gallon cold water.

Store all frozen fish at 0F (-20C). Use lean and moderate-fat fish within six months. High-fat fish should be used within three months.

If fish will be frozen no more than one to two months, wrap in moisture- and vapor-proof paper or heavy foil. If it will be frozen three to six months, *ice-packing* or *ice-glazing* protects against moisture loss. Ice-packing is suitable for small fish, such as trout. Large fish, such as salmon, take up less freezer space when ice-glazed.

To ice-pack fish, place small dressed or pan-dressed fish in plastic freezer containers or empty milk cartons. Fill containers to within 1/2 inch of top with water, then freeze solid.

To ice-glaze fish, freeze unwrapped fish on a baking sheet until solid. Then dip the fish in a bowl of ice water. An ice glaze will form over the fish. Return fish to the freezer for 15 to 20 minutes. Repeat dipping and freezing to build up a layer of ice 1/8 to 1/4 inch thick. To further protect the fish, wrap it in a moisture- and vapor-proof paper or heavy foil. Label and date the package, then store it in the freezer.

Wrap ice-glazed fillets and steaks in heavy foil with two layers of waxed paper between each piece. Don't forget to freeze bones, heads and trimmings to make fish stock.

Caring for the Catch

The freshest fish are those you catch yourself and cook within minutes or hours. To keep fish in prime condition, gut and bleed the fish and remove gills as soon as possible. This eliminates the largest source of bacterial contamination. Chill the fish on ice or refrigerate. Freeze, if desired. See left column for directions for freezing fish at home.

Cleaning Fish—Regardless of the way you cook whole fish, it must first be cleaned. This means removing gills and viscera. In some cases, you'll want to remove the scales and fins. When you purchase fish at the market, the retailer often will clean the fish for you.

Gutting a Roundfish—Roundfish can be gutted through the belly or through the gills. Fish markets gut most fish through the belly. It's the quickest method, and is suitable when you plan to stuff the fish or cut it into steaks or fillets. However, when you're cooking a small whole fish, such as trout or butterfish, it keeps its shape better when the viscera is removed through the gills.

To gut through the belly, open the belly cavity by making a straight incision from the anal opening to the jaw, being careful not to pierce the viscera. If there are eggs—called *roe*—remove them without breaking the membrane casing. To use roe, see page 84. Remove the viscera, then run the knife down both sides of the backbone to puncture the blood pockets. Lift the gill cover and cut or pull out the accordion-shape gill. Rinse the fish thoroughly under cool running water.

To gut through the gills, use the thumb of your left hand to open the gill covering. With the other hand, pull or cut out the accordion-shape gill and attached viscera. Thoroughly rinse the fish under cool running water, removing any remaining viscera.

Gutting a Flatfish—The organs of a flatfish occupy only a small part of the body cavity close to the gill. Cut off the head and viscera cavity, if desired. Rinse the fish under cool running water. When leaving the head on, make a small incision behind the gills and pull out the viscera. Rinse fish thoroughly.

Scales and fins don't need to be removed if the fish will be filleted or the skin will be removed

FISH ANATOMY

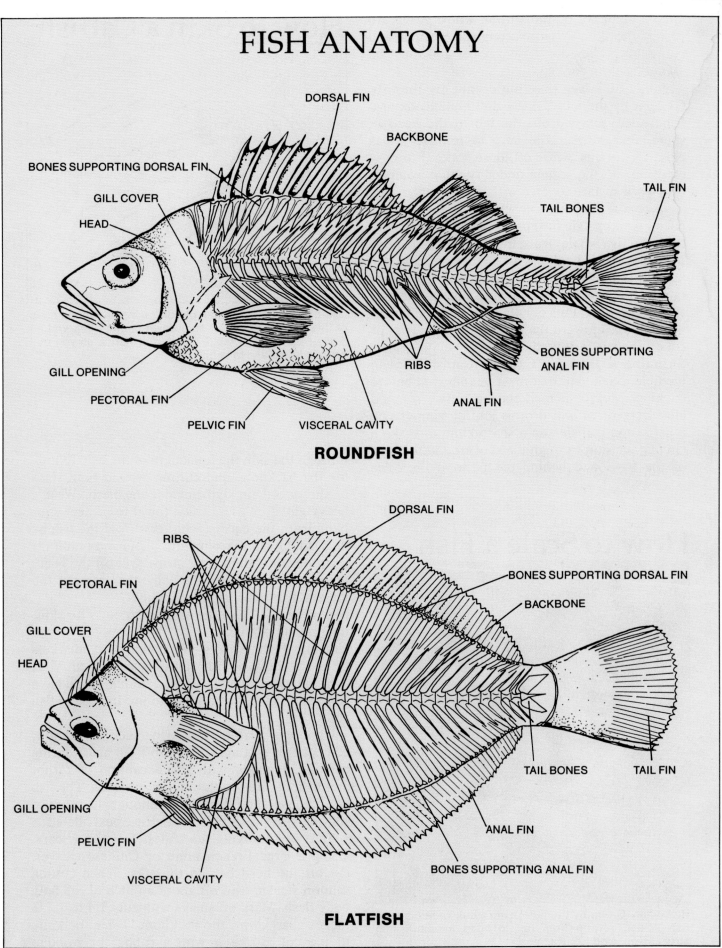

ROUNDFISH

FLATFISH

after cooking, or on most trout, whose scales are part of the skin. Other exceptions are catfish and eel, below. They don't have scales and must be skinned before cooking.

To remove scales, rinse but do not dry the fish. Grasp it by the tail. Using a dull knife blade or a fish scaler, scrape from the tail to the head in short, firm strokes. Be sure to remove scales close to the fins. Rinse off loose scales. For easy clean-up, do the scaling under running water or on a work surface covered with newspaper.

To remove fins, use kitchen shears to cut away pectoral and pelvic fins, page 8. When you plan to cook the fish whole, leave the dorsal and anal fins on. They help hold the flesh together and are pulled out easily after cooking. When steaking or boning fish, cut the flesh on both sides of the anal and dorsal fins. Pull out the fins and their connected bones toward the head of the fish. Trim or cut off the tail, if desired.

Skinning & Dressing Catfish—Catfish have an inedible tough skin that must be removed before cooking. Most fish markets sell catfish skinned and dressed, or will do this job for you. If you must skin a catfish, use a sharp knife to make a circular incision through the skin around the base of the head and behind the pectoral fin. Slice

How to Skin a Catfish

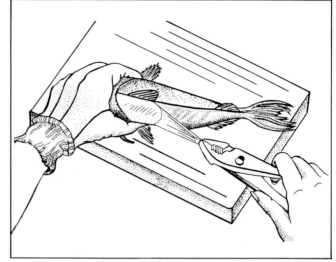

Use a sharp knife to cut a circular incision around base of head, behind fin. Cut skin down center back and on sides from head to tail. Protect your hands as you pull off skin from head to tail.

How to Scale a Fish

Rinse fish. Grasp by the tail. Using a dull knife blade or fish scaler, scrape from tail to head in short, firm strokes. Rinse off loose scales.

through the skin the full length of the fish, following the backbone and cutting around both sides of the dorsal fin. Do not cut the flesh. Wear a heavy glove or use a thick towel to protect your hand from the barbed whiskers. Hold the fish by its head. Grasp the skin with pliers and pull it off from head to tail in large strips. Cut off the head, fins and tail. Cut open the belly, then remove the viscera. Rinse the fish thoroughly.

Skinning Eel—Use the same method as for skinning catfish, above.

Cutting Fish Steaks—Although fish markets offer a variety of fish steaks, you can cut your own to desired thickness. As a bonus, you'll have the head, tail and trimmings to use in making fish stock.

Choose a firm-texture fish, such as salmon, cod, catfish or tuna, that won't fall apart during cooking. Flatfish, with the exception of turbot and halibut, are too thin to cut in steaks. The fish you choose should be large enough to produce serving-size steaks. Smaller fish are best filleted.

Start by removing the scales, fins and viscera. Using a large French knife or Chinese cleaver, cut off the head behind the gills. When cutting salmon steaks, trim off about an inch of the fatty belly flesh. Mark off steaks with cuts 3/4 to 1-1/2 inches apart down the backbone. Place the knife in the cut. Strike it with a rubber or wooden

How to Fillet Flatfish

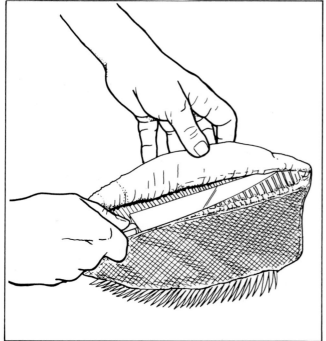

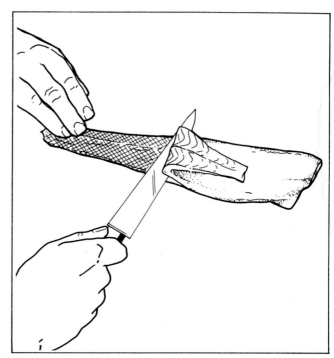

1/Starting at head, cut through flesh to backbone. Use long, smooth, cutting strokes from head to tail to separate flesh from bones. Turn fish over and repeat process.

2/Starting at the narrow end of fillet, pull skin taut. As you draw blade of filleting knife toward large end of fillet, separate flesh from skin.

mallet, if necessary, to force the knife through the bones and to ensure a clean cut through the flesh and backbone. Leave the skin and bones intact to help hold the flesh together during cooking. They can be removed easily after cooking.

Filleting Fish

To fillet roundfish, use a filleting knife, page 31. Cut off pectoral and pelvic fins, page 8. Leave anal and dorsal fins attached. If the skin will be left on, scale the fish, page 10. Place the fish on its side, with the backbone toward you. Make a shallow cut crosswise to the backbone at the tail-end and a shallow cut diagonally behind the gills. It is not necessary to remove the head or tail. Cut along the center back from head to tail, deep enough to expose the backbone. With long, smooth cutting strokes, separate the upper fillet from the bones. Trim ragged edges. Turn the fish over and repeat the process. Remove small bones with your fingers, tweezers or needle-nose pliers.

To fillet a flatfish, place dark-side up on a work surface, tail-end toward you. *To cut a single*

fillet from each side, use a filleting knife to cut across the body, below the gill, cutting to the bones. Score both sides of the fish where the ribs and fin bones mesh, making an outline of the fillet. Cut across the tail, cutting to the bones. Start at the head and use long, smooth strokes to separate the flesh from the ribs. Lift off the fillet. Repeat on the other side. Trim ragged edges.

To cut four fillets from a large fish, cut midway between dorsal and anal fins, deep enough to expose the backbone. Start at the head and use long, smooth strokes to separate the flesh from the ribs, cutting toward the anal fin. Cut the skin loose at the anal fin. Cut off the fillet at the tail end. Trim ragged edges. Repeat with other fillet, cutting toward dorsal fin. Turn fish over and repeat cutting bottom fillets.

To skin fillets, place skin-side down on a work surface. Starting at the narrow end of the fillet and holding the blade almost horizontal, use a filleting knife to separate the skin and flesh. Pull the skin taut as you draw the blade toward the large end of the fillet.

SALTWATER FISH

The following is a compendium of common saltwater fish available in U.S. and Canadian markets.

Species or Family *Other Names*	Varieties *Other Names*	Fat Content & Texture	Cooking & Serving Suggestions	Average Market Size	Forms Available	Comments
Anchovy		High fat Fine texture	Appetizers Salads Dips	4 to 6 in.	Whole Salted fillets Canned flat rolled	Occasionally, anchovies are available fresh. Most are filleted, cured in salt and olive oil, then canned. They are sold rolled or flat.
Angler *Baudroie* *Bellyfish* *Frogfish* *Goosefish* *Lotte* *Monkfish* *Sea Devil*		Low fat Firm texture	Poach, Steam Bake Broil, Grill Fry, Sauté Soups, Stews	2 to 25 lbs.	Boneless tail Fillets	Only the thick, tapered tail section is edible; the head is usually discarded at sea. Angler's firm, white flesh has a mild, sweet flavor somewhat like lobster.
Barracuda, Pacific *California* *Barracuda*		Moderate fat Firm texture	Poach, Steam Bake Broil, Grill Fry, Sauté Soups, Stews	4 to 8 lbs.	Whole Dressed Fillets	Great barracuda is often toxic, but Pacific barracuda has an excellent flavor and can be interchanged with mahi mahi or wahoo.
Bluefish *Blue Runner*		High fat Fine, soft texture	Bake Broil, Grill	3 to 6 lbs.	Whole Dressed Fillets	Bluefish does not freeze well. Fillets have a strip of dark flesh running down the center that can have a strong fishy flavor. To remove, cut a shallow V along both sides of the dark strip, being careful not to cut completely through the flesh. Lift out and discard dark strip.
Bonito (See Tuna)						
Butterfish *Dollarfish* *Pacific* *Pompano* *Pomfret*		High fat Fine texture	Bake Broil, Grill Fry, Sauté	1/4 to 1 lb.	Whole Smoked	Because butterfish are so small, most are cooked whole. Do not confuse butterfish with sablefish, which is often called butterfish and sold as fillets.
Cod	Atlantic Cod	Low fat Firm texture	Poach, Steam Bake Broil, Grill Fry, Sauté Soups, Stews	10 to 25 lbs.	Fillets Steaks Salted Smoked	Cod is the staple of the Canadian and New England fishing industry, and is one of the most abundant and widely available fish. Much of it is frozen aboard fishing boats.
	Pacific Cod *True Cod*	Low fat Firm texture	Poach, Steam Bake Broil, Grill Fry, Sauté Soups, Stews	5 to 10 lbs.	Whole Dressed Fillets Steaks	Pacific cod is almost identical to Atlantic cod. Black cod, rock cod and lingcod are not of the same species. See Sablefish, Rockfish and Lingcod.
	Scrod	Low fat Firm texture	Bake Fry, Sauté	Under 2-1/2 lbs.	Whole Dressed Fillets	Scrod is young cod or haddock weighing under 2-1/2 lbs. It is considered a delicacy.
Corbina (See Drum/Croaker)						
Croaker (See Drum/Croaker)						

Species or Family *Other Names*	Varieties *Other Names*	Fat Content & Texture	Cooking & Serving Suggestions	Average Market Size	Forms Available	Comments
Cusk		Low fat Firm texture	Poach, Steam Bake Broil, Grill Fry, Sauté Soups, Stews	1-1/2 to 5 lbs.	Whole Fillets	Cusk is not well known but is gaining in popularity. It looks and tastes similar to cod.
Drum/ Croaker	Atlantic Croaker *Crocus Golden Croaker Grodin Hardhead*	Low fat Firm texture	Poach, Steam Bake Broil, Grill Fry, Sauté Soups, Stews	1/2 to 2 lbs.	Whole Dressed Fillets	Drum represents a large and diverse family of fish found in temperate and tropical waters. Some are known as *croakers* because of a characteristic drumming or croaking noise they make.
	Black Drum	Low fat Firm texture	Poach, Steam Bake Broil, Grill Fry, Sauté Soups, Stews	2 to 10 lbs.	Whole Dressed Fillets Steaks	A popular fish for making chowder.
	Corbina *Corvina*	Moderate fat Firm texture	Poach, Steam Bake Broil, Grill	3 to 7 lbs.	Whole Dressed Fillets	Corbina is caught primarily off the California-Baja coast.
	Kingfish	Low fat Firm texture	Poach, Steam Bake Broil, Grill Fry, Sauté Soups, Stews	1/2 to 2 lbs.	Whole Dressed	Do not confuse this kingfish with king mackerel, which is also called *kingfish.*
	Redfish *Channel Bass Red Drum*	Low fat Firm texture	Poach, steam Bake Broil, Grill Fry, Sauté Soups, Stews	3 to 30 lbs. (3 to 6 lbs. preferred)	Whole Dressed Fillets	Redfish was popularized by New Orleans chefs.
	Spot	Low fat Firm texture	Bake Broil, Grill Fry, Sauté	1/4 to 1-1/4 lbs.	Whole Dressed	Because of its small size, spot is usually pan-fried.
Eel		High fat Firm texture	Bake Soups, Stews	Up to 3 feet long	Whole Smoked	Eel is a snake-like fish that is much more popular in Europe and Japan than in the U.S. and Canada. It has a tough skin that must be removed before cooking.
Flounder/Sole						Flounder and sole are the best-known fish in the U.S. and Canada. They are prized for their delicate flavor and fine texture. All of the so-called soles, with the exception of European Dover sole, are actually varieties of flounder. However, flounder and sole are cooked by the same methods. Although they differ somewhat in taste, texture and price, most varieties of flounder and sole can be interchanged in recipes.
	American Plaice *Dab Canadian Plaice*	Low fat Fine texture	Poach, Steam Bake, Broil Fry, Sauté	2 to 3 lbs.	Whole Dressed Fillets	One of the most common and commercially important Atlantic flatfish.

Species or Family *Other Names*	Varieties *Other Names*	Fat Content & Texture	Cooking & Serving Suggestions	Average Market Size	Forms Available	Comments
Flounder/Sole (cont.)	Butter Sole	Low fat Fine texture	Poach, Steam Bake, Broil Fry, Sauté	1/2 to 2 lbs.	Whole Dressed Fillets	Butter sole is found almost exclusively in Western markets.
	English Sole *Lemon Sole*	Low fat Fine texture	Poach, Steam Bake, Broil Fry, Sauté	1/4 to 2 lbs.	Whole Dressed Fillets	A plentiful species often marketed in Western U.S. and Canada as *fillet of sole.*
	Fluke *Summer Flounder*	Low fat Fine texture	Poach, Steam Bake, Broil Fry, Sauté	2 to 5 lbs.	Whole Dressed Fillets	Fluke comes from both Atlantic and Pacific waters and is larger than most other flatfish. It has a large mouth and sharp teeth.
	Gray Sole *Witch Flounder*	Low fat Fine texture	Poach, Steam Bake, Broil Fry, Sauté	2 to 7 lbs.	Whole Dressed Fillets	Gray sole gets its name from its grayish upper skin.
	Pacific Dover Sole	Low fat Fine texture	Poach, Steam Bake, Broil Fry, Sauté	1-1/2 to 4 lbs.	Whole Dressed Fillets	This fish has a delicate flavor and texture.
	Petrale Sole *Brill Sole*	Low fat Fine texture	Poach, Steam Bake, Broil Fry, Sauté	1 to 5 lbs.	Whole Dressed Fillets	The most expensive Pacific sole with a fine flavor and texture.
	Rex Sole	Low fat Fine texture	Poach, Steam Bake, Broil Fry, Sauté	1/2 to 1 lb.	Whole Dressed Fillets	Another Pacific variety with a fine flavor and texture.
	Sand Dab	Low fat Fine texture	Poach, Steam Bake, Broil Fry, Sauté	1/2 to 3/4 lb.	Whole Dressed	A prized fish with a sweet flavor and fine, delicate texture.
	Sand Sole	Low fat Fine texture	Poach, Steam Bake, Broil Fry, Sauté	1 to 3 lbs.	Whole Dressed Fillets	As with other members of the sole family, serve with a delicate sauce, such as Beurre Blanc, page 146.
	Starry Flounder	Low fat Fine texture	Poach, Steam Bake, Broil Fry, Sauté	2 to 10 lbs.	Whole Dressed Fillets	See comments for sand sole. Starry flounder is caught from central California to Alaska.
	Winter Flounder *Flounder Blackback Flounder Lemon Sole*	Low fat Fine texture	Poach, Steam Bake, Broil Fry, Sauté	1 to 5 lbs.	Whole Dressed Fillets	This is the most abundant and popular flounder sold. It is usually marketed simply as *flounder.*
	Yellowtail Flounder	Low fat Fine texture	Poach, Steam Bake, Broil Fry, Sauté	1/2 to 2 lbs.	Whole Dressed Fillets	This fish is characterized by a yellow tail and an olive-brown skin dotted with rusty spots.
Grouper *Sea Bass*	Black Grouper Gag Nassau Grouper Red Grouper Yellowfin Grouper	Low fat Firm texture	Poach, Steam Bake Broil, Grill Fry, Sauté Soups, Stews	3 to 25 lbs.	Whole Dressed Fillets Steaks	Grouper is sometimes sold as *sea bass.* It can be used interchangeably with sea bass. The skin of most groupers is tough and should be removed before cooking. See Sea Bass, page 18.

Species or Family *Other Names*	Varieties *Other Names*	Fat Content & Texture	Cooking & Serving Suggestions	Average Market Size	Forms Available	Comments
Haddock		Low fat Firm texture	Poach, Steam Bake Broil, Grill Fry, Sauté Soups, Stews	3 to 5 lbs.	Whole Dressed Fillets Steaks Smoked	Haddock is closely related to cod, though it is usually smaller. It can be used interchangeably in recipes. Haddock is available fresh and frozen. Smoked haddock is known as *finnan haddie.*
	Scrod	Low fat Firm texture	Bake Fry, Sauté	Under 2-1/2 lbs.	Whole Dressed Fillets	Scrod is young cod or haddock weighing under 2-1/2 lbs. It is considered a delicacy.
Hake (also see Whiting)		Low fat Firm texture	Poach, Steam Bake Broil, Grill Fry, Sauté Soups, Stews	1 to 8 lbs.	Fillets Steaks Cured	This mild-flavored Atlantic fish is caught in the summer and early fall. Although related to cod, it is often less expensive than cod.
Halibut	California Halibut	Low fat Firm texture	Poach, Steam Bake Broil, Grill Fry, Sauté Soups, Stews	5 to 20 lbs.	Whole Fillets Steaks	This popular flatfish is caught all year off the southern California coast.
	Pacific Halibut	Low fat Firm texture	Poach, Steam Bake Broil, Grill Fry, Sauté Soups, Stews	5 to 60 lbs.	Whole Dressed Steaks	This high-quality fish has a finer texture and firmer flesh than California halibut. Due to over-fishing, commercial fishing is carefully regulated.
Herring		High fat Fine, soft texture	Appetizers Salads Dips	1/4 to 1 lb.	Whole Pickled Salted Smoked	Some herring is available fresh, but it is usually sold pickled, salted and smoked. The flesh is soft-textured when fresh, but with pickling and smoking, becomes more firm. Some forms are listed below. Others are available as hard salted herring, marinated herring and herring in sour-cream sauce.
			Appetizers		Bismarck Herring	Fillets pickled in vinegar, sugar, salt and onions.
			Appetizers		Rollmops	Fillets of Bismarck herring rolled around onion or pickle slices and preserved in vinegar and spices.
			Appetizers		Schmalz Herring	Pieces of mature herring, preserved in brine.
			Appetizers		Maatjes Herring	Young herring, filleted, skinned and cured in sugar, vinegar and spices. Typically, it has a reddish color.
			Appetizers		Kippered Herring	High-fat, mature herring that are split, salted and cold-smoked. A classic for British breakfasts.
Lingcod		Low fat Firm texture	Poach, Steam Bake Broil, Grill Fry, Sauté Soups, Stews	3 to 20 lbs.	Whole Dressed Fillets Steaks	Lingcod is not actually cod, but a member of the greenling family. Greenling is only sold under other names. Its firm-texture flesh is lean and mild, like cod.

Species or Family *Other Names*	Varieties *Other Names*	Fat Content & Texture	Cooking & Serving Suggestions	Average Market Size	Forms Available	Comments
Mackerel	Atlantic Mackerel *Boston Mackerel*	High fat Firm texture	Bake Broil, Grill	1/2 to 2-1/2 lbs.	Whole Fillets Smoked Canned	This beautiful, brilliant-colored fish is relatively inexpensive. It is well liked in Europe and is becoming accepted in the U.S. and Canada.
	King Mackerel *Kingfish*	High fat Firm texture	Bake Broil, Grill	5 to 25 lbs.	Fillets Steaks Canned Smoked	This high-fat mackerel has a strong flavor.
	Pacific Jack	High fat Firm texture	Bake Broil, Grill	1/2 to 2-1/2 lbs.	Whole Canned Smoked	Use an assertive sauce with this flavorful fish.
	Spanish Mackerel	High fat Firm texture	Bake Broil, Grill	1-1/2 to 4 lbs.	Whole Canned	This delicately flavored fish is considered one of the finest mackerel available.
	Wahoo *Ono*	Moderate to high fat Firm texture	Bake Broil, Grill	20 to 30 lbs.	Steaks Fillets	Wahoo is considered a fine-eating fish. Its mild flavor is similar to albacore.
Mahi Mahi *Dolphin Fish* *Dorado*		Moderate fat Firm texture	Poach, Steam Bake Broil, Grill Fry, Sauté Soups, Stews	2 to 40 lbs.	Steaks Fillets	Do not confuse dolphin fish with the mammal dolphin. The edible dolphin fish is usually sold under its Hawaiian name, mahi mahi.
Mullet *Striped Mullet* *Lisa* *Silver Mullet*		Moderate to high fat Firm texture	Bake Broil, Grill Fry, Sauté	1/2 to 4 lbs.	Whole Fillets	Fat content varies with the season caught. Mullet has a mild nut-like flavor. *Red mullet* is from Europe and is not of the same family.
Ocean Perch, Atlantic *Redfish* *Red Perch* *Rosefish*		Low fat Firm texture	Poach, Steam Bake Broil, Grill Fry, Sauté Soups, Stews	1/2 to 2 lbs.	Whole Fillets	Perch is marketed fresh and frozen. Most is exported from Iceland, Canada and Greenland.
Orange Roughy		Low fat Firm texture	Poach, Steam Bake Broil, Grill Fry, Sauté Soups, Stews	2 to 5 lbs.	Fillets	This New Zealand fish was recently introduced to the U.S. and Canada. Its snow-white flesh tastes similar to sole, but is less expensive.
Pollock	Atlantic Pollock *Blue Cod* *Boston Bluefish*	Low to moderate fat Firm texture	Poach, Steam Bake Broil, Grill Fry, Sauté Soups, Stews	4 to 12 lbs.	Whole Dressed Fillets Steaks	Pollock is closely related to cod, though it is usually smaller. It is cooked the same as cod.
	Alaska Pollock *Snow Cod* *Walleye Pollock*	Low fat Firm texture	Poach, Steam Bake Broil, Grill Fry, Sauté Soups, Stews	1 to 4 lbs.	Fillets	Most is frozen aboard fishing boats. It has a slightly sweet flavor.
Pompano		Moderate fat Firm texture	Poach, Steam Bake Broil, Grill Fry, Sauté Soups, Stews	3/4 to 3 lbs.	Whole Dressed Fillets	Considered one of the finest eating fish, pompano is very expensive.

Species or Family *Other Names*	Varieties *Other Names*	Fat Content & Texture	Cooking & Serving Suggestions	Average Market Size	Forms Available	Comments
Porgy Scup		Low fat Firm texture	Bake Broil, Grill Fry, Sauté	1/2 to 2 lbs.	Whole Dressed	This New England fish is gaining in popularity as a food and sports fish in the U.S. and Canada.
Redfish (See Drum/Croaker)						
Red Snapper		Low fat Firm texture	Poach, Steam Bake Broil, Grill Fry, Sauté Soups, Stews	2 to 8 lbs.	Whole Dressed Fillets	Red snapper is identified by its vivid rose-pink skin and red eyes. It is an Atlantic and Gulf Coast fish.
Rockfish *Rock Cod* *Pacific Red Snapper* *Pacific Snapper* *Pacific Ocean Perch*		Low fat Firm texture	Poach, Steam Bake Broil, Grill Fry, Sauté Soups, Stews	1 to 5 lbs.	Whole Dressed Fillets	There are more than 50 varieties in a rainbow of colors. Because of the market appeal of red snapper, rockfish are often sold under the name *Pacific snapper.* However, they are not a Pacific counterpart of the real Atlantic red snapper.
Sablefish *Alaska Cod* *Black Cod* *Butterfish*		High fat Fine, soft texture	Bake, Broil Fry, Sauté	1 to 10 lbs.	Whole Dressed Fillets Steaks Cold- smoked	Because of its high oil content, sablefish is excellent for smoking. It is marketed as smoked black cod or smoked Alaska cod. It can be served thinly sliced like smoked salmon.
Salmon						Six different species of salmon are available commercially, five of which are found in the Pacific. More than 90% come from Alaskan waters; 50% of the catch is canned.
	Atlantic Salmon	High fat Firm texture	Poach, Steam Bake Broil, Grill Fry, Sauté	7 to 12 lbs.	Steaks Fillets Smoked	Atlantic salmon makes superb smoked fish because of its high-fat content. Canada exports a large quantity.
	Chum Salmon *Keta*	Low to moderate fat Firm texture	Poach, Steam Bake Broil, Grill Fry, Sauté	7 to 9 lbs.	Whole Dressed Steaks Fillets Smoked Canned	Chum Salmon is fished from Puget Sound to Arctic Alaska. It is the lightest in color and the least fatty of the salmons.
	Coho Salmon *Silver Salmon*	High fat Firm texture	Poach, Steam Bake Broil, Grill Fry, Sauté	3 to 12 lbs.	Whole Dressed Steaks Fillets Smoked	Coho salmon flesh is light to dark-pink or orange-red. It is considered choice for smoking.
	King Salmon *Chinook*	High fat Firm texture	Poach, Steam Bake Broil, Grill Fry, Sauté	5 to 30 lbs.	Whole Dressed Steaks Fillets Smoked Cured Canned	One of the most commercially valuable fish in the world. Flesh color ranges from deep-salmon to almost white. It is excellent for smoking.

Species or Family *Other Names*	Varieties *Other Names*	Fat Content & Texture	Cooking & Serving Suggestions	Average Market Size	Forms Available	Comments
Salmon (cont.)	Pink Salmon *Humpback*	Moderate fat Firm texture	Poach, Steam Bake Broil, Grill Fry, Sauté	2 to 8 lbs.	Most is canned Whole Dressed	This is the smallest and the most abundant of the Pacific salmon.
	Sockeye Salmon *Red Salmon*	High fat Firm texture	Poach, Steam Bake Broil, Grill Fry, Sauté	3 to 12 lbs.	Whole Dressed Fillets Steaks Canned Smoked	Sockeye salmon is prized for its deep-red flesh.
Sardine		High fat Soft, fine texture	Appetizers Salads Dips	2 to 4 inches	Most is canned; Some sold whole	Sardines are canned in oil, tomato sauce or mustard. Some are smoked. Norwegian bristling sardines are the finest quality, but Maine sardines are good quality and less expensive.
Scrod (See Cod or Haddock)						
Sea Bass	Black Sea Bass	Moderate fat Firm texture	Poach, Steam Bake Broil, Grill Fry, Sauté Soups, Stews	1-1/2 to 5 lbs.	Whole Dressed Fillets Steaks	Black sea bass varies in color from smoky grey to brown. It has white, firm flesh with a mild flavor.
	White Sea Bass *Sea Bass*	Moderate fat Firm texture	Poach, Steam Bake Broil, Grill Fry, Sauté Soups, Stews	10 to 40 lbs.	Whole Dressed Fillets Steaks Smoked	White sea bass is sold simply as *sea bass* in most markets.
Sea Trout *Gray* *Silver* *Spotted* *White*		Moderate fat Firm texture	Poach, Steam Bake Broil, Grill Fry, Sauté Soups, Stews	1 to 6 lbs.	Whole Dressed Fillets	All four species of sea trout are caught commercially by Southeastern U.S. fishermen.
Shad		High fat Fine texture	Bake Broil, Grill Fry, Sauté	3 to 4 lbs.	Whole Boned Fillets	Shad is a difficult fish to bone and is usually sold as fillets. The roe of the female is considered a delicacy.
Shark	Leopard Mako Pacific Blue Soup Fin Thresher	Low fat Firm, dense texture	Poach, Steam Bake Broil, Grill Fry, Sauté	15 to over 100 lbs.	Steaks Chunks	Serve an assertive sauce with this flavorful, meat-like fish. Shark is gaining in popularity as a food.
Sheepshead (also see Sheepshead under Freshwater Fish)		Moderate fat Firm texture	Poach, Steam Bake Broil, Grill Fry, Sauté Soups, Stews	3/4 to 8 lbs.	Whole Dressed Fillets	Sheepshead's name comes from its large, hammer-shape head. It has dark vertical bars that run down its sides.
Skate *Ray*		Low fat Firm texture	Bake Fry, Sauté	Wings weigh 1 to 5 lbs.	Wings Skinless wings	This odd fish is shaped like a kite, with wing-like pectoral fins and a long, thick tail. The wings, which are the part eaten, have a delicate flavor similar to that of scallops.

SALTWATER FISH, continued

Species or Family *Other Names*	Varieties *Other Names*	Fat Content & Texture	Cooking & Serving Suggestions	Average Market Size	Forms Available	Comments
Smelt (See Freshwater Fish)						
Sole (See Flounder)						
Spot (See Drum/Croaker)						
Striped Bass		Moderate fat Firm texture	Poach, Steam Bake Broil, Grill Fry, Sauté Soups, Stews	2 to 15 lbs.	Whole Dressed Fillets Steaks	This Atlantic fish is a member of the sea bass family. It is one of the most valuable fish in North America.
Sturgeon (See Freshwater Fish)						
Swordfish		Low to moderate fat Firm, dense texture	Poach, Steam Bake Broil, Grill Fry, Sauté	100 to 200 lbs.	Steaks Chunks	Swordfish is caught in the Atlantic, Pacific and Gulf of Mexico. Its flavor is not as strong as shark.
Tilefish *Tile Bass*		Low fat Firm texture	Poach, Steam Bake Broil, Grill Fry, Sauté Soups, Stews	2 to 30 lbs.	Whole Dressed Fillets Steaks	This relatively unknown fish tastes similar to, and can be cooked like, rockfish.
Tuna	Albacore	High fat Firm texture	Bake Broil, Grill	10 to 60 lbs.	Dressed Fillets Steaks Canned	Only albacore tuna can be called *white* or *white-meat* tuna. The remaining species fall under *light-meat* or *dark-meat* tuna.
	Bluefin	High fat Firm texture	Bake Broil, Grill	Up to 1000 lbs.	Dressed Steaks Canned	Canned tuna may be packed in water, vegetable oil or olive oil. When packed in olive oil, it is sometimes called *Tonno*.
	Bonito	Moderate to high fat Firm texture	Bake Broil, Grill	1-1/2 to 5 lbs.	Whole Steaks Fillets Canned	Bonito is less expensive than other tuna. It is also less flavorful. When canned, it is not labeled *tuna*.
	Skipjack	High fat Firm texture	Bake Broil, Grill	4 to 24 lbs.	Canned	Serve with a moderate or assertive sauce.
	Yellowfin	High fat Firm texture	Bake Broil, Grill	30 to 150 lbs.	Steaks Canned	Serve a moderate or assertive sauce with yellowfin.
Turbot *Greenland Turbot Greenland Halibut*		Low fat Firm texture	Poach, Steam Bake, Broil Fry, Sauté	8 to 25 lbs.	Fillets	Like halibut and flounder, turbot is a flatfish.
Whiting *Silver Hake*		Low fat Firm texture	Poach, Steam Bake Broil, Grill Fry, Sauté Soups, Stews	3/4 to 5 lbs.	Whole Dressed Fillets	Whiting is related to hake. It comes from cold North Atlantic waters.

FRESHWATER FISH

The following is a compendium of common freshwater fish available in U.S. and Canadian markets.

Species or Family *Other Names*	Varieties *Other Names*	Fat Content & Texture	Cooking & Serving Suggestions	Average Market Size	Forms Available	Comments
Buffalofish		Moderate fat Firm texture	Poach, Steam Bake Broil, Grill Fry, Sauté Soups, Stews	2 to 8 lbs.	Whole Dressed Fillets Smoked	This southern favorite is caught in the Mississippi and its tributaries, and in the Great Lakes.
Carp		Low to moderate fat Firm texture	Poach, Steam Bake Broil, Grill Fry, Sauté Soups, Stews	2 to 8 lbs.	Whole Dressed Fillets	This was the first fish to be aquacultured centuries ago in China. It is strongly identified with central European and Chinese cuisines.
Catfish *Channel Catfish*		Low fat Firm texture	Poach, Steam Bake Broil, Grill Fry, Sauté Soups, Stews	Aqua-cultured: 1/2 to 3 lbs. Caught wild: 1 to 6 lbs.	Whole Dressed Head and skin off Fillets	Most catfish are aquacultured; 70% are harvested in Mississippi. Wild catfish are caught in the Great Lakes, other lakes and inland rivers. There are 20 species of freshwater catfish, but channel catfish is the main commercial species, and considered the best eating. About half the catfish produced are frozen. Catfish have a tough skins that must be removed, page 10.

Eel
(See Eel under Saltwater Fish)

Species or Family *Other Names*	Varieties *Other Names*	Fat Content & Texture	Cooking & Serving Suggestions	Average Market Size	Forms Available	Comments
Lake Herring		High fat Firm texture	Bake Broil, Grill	1/2 to 1 lb.	Whole Dressed Smoked	Lake herring resemble saltwater herring in appearance and flavor.
Perch	White Perch	Low fat Firm texture	Poach, Steam Bake Broil, Grill Fry, Sauté Soups, Stews	1 to 4 lbs.	Whole Dressed	Because of their size, most perch are pan-fried, but can be prepared by all other methods. Perch are an important commercial and sports fish.
	Yellow Perch *Lake Perch*	Low fat Firm texture	Poach, Steam Bake Broil, Grill Fry, Sauté Soups, Stews	1/4 to 3/4 lb.	Whole Dressed Fillets Butterfly fillets	See comments for white perch.
Pike	Northern Pike *Lake Pickerel* *Grass Pike*	Low fat Firm texture	Poach, Steam Bake Broil, Grill Fry, Sauté	2 to 10 lbs.	Whole Dressed Fillets	Supplies have been depleted and in many places Northern pike is no longer caught commercially. Today, it is primarily a sports fish.
	Walleye Pike	Low fat Firm texture	Poach, Steam Bake Broil, Grill Fry, Sauté	1 to 3 lbs.	Whole Dressed Fillets	Walleye pike is considered one of the best-eating freshwater fish available.

FRESHWATER FISH, continued

Species or Family *Other Names*	Varieties *Other Names*	Fat Content & Texture	Cooking & Serving Suggestions	Average Market Size	Forms Available	Comments
Trout (also see Sea Trout under Saltwater Fish)	Lake Trout	Moderate to high fat Firm texture	Poach, Steam Bake Broil, Grill Fry, Sauté	2 to 8 lbs.	Dressed Smoked	Lake trout is the largest trout caught in U.S. and Canadian waters.
	Rainbow Trout	Moderate to high fat Firm texture	Poach, Steam Bake Broil, Grill Fry, Sauté	Aquacultured: 5 oz. to 1 lb.	Dressed Smoked Boned & butterflied Smoked	Rainbow trout and trout are virtually synonymous. All rainbow trout sold commercially are farm-raised. Trout do not need to be scaled.
	Steelhead	Moderate to high fat Firm texture	Poach, Steam Bake Broil, Grill Fry, Sauté	6 to 35 lbs.	Whole Dressed	Steelheads are large rainbow trout, but are actually members of the salmon family. Their flavorful flesh is considered a delicacy.
Salmon (See Salmon under Saltwater Fish)						
Shad (See Shad under Saltwater Fish)						
Sheepshead (also see Sheepshead under Saltwater Fish)		Low fat Firm texture	Poach, Steam Bake Broil, Grill Fry, Sauté Soups, Stews	1 to 5 lbs.	Whole Dressed Fillets	This fish looks like its saltwater relative. Its name comes from the large hammer-like head. It is caught in lakes and rivers.
Smelt *White Bait*		Moderate to high fat Firm texture	Fry, Sauté	From 4 to 15 per lb.	Whole Dressed	Small smelt are pan-fried or deep-fried and eaten whole—head, bones, viscera and all. Larger smelt should be gutted and headed before eating.
Sturgeon	White Sturgeon *Pacific Sturgeon*	High fat Firm, dense texture	Bake Broil, Grill	8 to 1000 lbs.	Steaks Chunks Smoked	Sturgeon is the largest freshwater fish in the world. Due to the demand for its roe in making caviar, its commercial harvest is restricted in some parts of the world. Green sturgeon, a similar but fatter species, is generally smoked.
Whitefish		High fat Firm texture	Bake Broil, Grill	1-1/2 to 6 lbs.	Whole Dressed Fillets Steaks Smoked	This is one of the best-eating freshwater fish. Its roe may be cooked like shad roe, page 84.

Shellfish: 1. Cooked Pacific Rock Lobster; 2. Scallops; 3. Butter Clams; 4. Mussels; 5. Little Neck Clams; 6. Cooked Dungeness Crab; 7. Oysters; 8. Crayfish; 9. Squid; 10. Cooked American or Maine Lobster; 11. Shrimp; 12. Tiny Shrimp.

Shellfish Primer

There are two basic categories of shellfish used in cooking: *mollusks* and *crustaceans*. Mollusks have a soft body fully or partially enclosed in a shell. Scallops, oysters, clams, mussels, abalone and squid are mollusks. Crustaceans have elongated, segmented bodies with softer, jointed shells. Lobster, crab, shrimp, crayfish and langostinos fall into this category.

Selecting & Storing Shellfish—Shells of oysters, mussels and clams should be closed, or should close when tapped or pressed together. Except for soft-shell clams, a gaping shell that will not close indicates the mollusk is dead.

Live crab, lobster and crayfish should be active and heavy for their size. When cooked, the legs, claws and tail should be pulled in tight. This indicates the shellfish was alive when cooked. After cooking, if the crab legs are splayed out, or the tail of a lobster or crayfish is relaxed, it means the crustacean was dead or near death when it was cooked. Meat quality will not be as good as if it were cooked while alive and active.

Cover live shellfish with a damp cloth or paper towel and store in the refrigerator. Most shellfish live part of their lives out of water and will keep a day or more when stored this way. Do not store shellfish in fresh water because it will kill them.

Freezing Shellfish—If you freeze crab or lobster, cook them first, then remove the meat. To freeze clams and oysters, shuck them, opposite and page 28, then freeze them in their own juices. To freeze shrimp, remove their heads, then freeze them raw, in the shell.

Abalone

Abalone, one of the most prized shellfish, is found clinging to rocks along the California, Mexican and Japanese coastlines. Fresh abalone is increasingly rare due to over-fishing and natural predation. It is forbidden by law to ship abalone from California waters to other states. However, frozen abalone is widely available.

If you can get fresh abalone, the tough foot muscle, which is the edible portion, must be cleaned, trimmed, sliced and pounded into steaks, page 79. Frozen abalone can be purchased already sliced and pounded. These prepared steaks are ready to cook.

Clams

Three primary species of clams are harvested on a commercial basis: hard-shell, soft-shell and sea clams.

Hard-shell clams are the most valuable species available. More Atlantic hard-shell clams are marketed than any other. They are identified by size and where they're sold. Small hard-shell clams are known as *little necks,* and are most often served raw on the half-shell. Medium-size *cherry-stone* clams are usually steamed and baked, but are also served on the half-shell. The largest and cheapest hard-shell clams are called *quahogs, chowder hogs* or *chowder clams.* They are full-flavored and have a tougher texture than little necks and cherrystones. They are generally chopped for use in chowder, clam fritters and other mixed dishes.

Manila clams are the most common Pacific coast hard-shell clam. Most are farmed and marketed as *littlenecks*—spelled as one word in contrast to Atlantic little necks. *Butter* and *Pismo clams* are also Pacific hard-shell clams.

Soft-shell clams actually have thin, brittle shells, not soft shells. A soft-shell clam cannot close its shell tightly because its long neck, or *siphon,* extends beyond the shell. East Coast soft-shell clams are called *steamer, Ipswich, manninose, belly* and *mud clams.* They are usually served steamed or fried and are rarely eaten raw.

The Pacific Northwest is famous for the huge *geoduck clam,* pronounced *gooey-duck.* The geoduck is mostly neck and averages three pounds in weight, about half of which is edible.

Sea clams, also called *surf, beach, skimmers* and *bar clams,* make up the largest group of harvested clams. Most are chopped and minced for canning or used in prepared products.

Clams are marketed live in the shell, as fresh or frozen shucked meat, and canned. *Clam liquor,* also called *clam juice, clam broth* and *clam nectar,* is available canned or bottled.

When buying hard-shell clams in the shell, a tightly closed shell is the best indication that it's alive. If the shell is slightly open, tap it to see that the clam closes its shell. Discard any that don't close. In the case of a soft-shell clam that can't close its shell, touch the neck to see if it twitches. Refrigerate clams, but do not put them in fresh water.

Clam digging is a popular sport on many coastlines. Different regions have different regulations regarding daily limits, approved methods of digging and seasons when it's safe to take

How to Open Clams

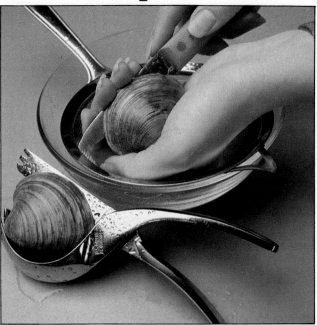

Holding clam over a bowl, insert a thin paring knife or clam knife between shells. Do not wiggle knife. Run knife blade around shell halves to sever muscles holding shells together.

them. Contact your local fisheries department for information.

If you've dug a bucketful of clams, you must *purge* them of sand and mud before cooking. **To purge clams,** let the clams stand 15 to 20 minutes in clear sea water. Or, make a solution of 1/3 cup salt to 1 gallon water. Clams will die in fresh water. Change the water and repeat the soaking process 2 or 3 times. Scrub shells thoroughly with a stiff-bristle brush. Clams bought at fish markets have already been purged and only need to have their shells scrubbed.

Soft-shell clams are easiest to open because they do not have tight-fitting shells. If you place hard-shell clams in the freezer for 5 to 10 minutes, their muscles will relax, making them easier to open. Open clams over a strainer placed in a bowl to strain and catch the *clam liquor,* so it can be used for cooking.

To open a clam, insert a thin paring knife or clam knife between the shells without wiggling the knife, which may cause the shells to crack. Run the knife blade around the shell halves to sever the muscles holding them together. Cut the clam free of the bottom shell and remove any grit or bits of shell. Strain clam liquor into a bowl. For **clams on-the-half-shell,** place the clam with its liquor in the bottom shell; discard the top shell. Serve with lemon wedges and freshly ground pepper.

How to Clean Cooked Dungeness Crab

1/Place your thumb under the shell at midpoint and pull firmly. Cut off face; pull out and discard bile sac.

2/Turn crab on its back. Remove apron; pull out and discard feathery gills. Save creamy crab fat.

Crab

Blue crab is the major commercial catch along the Atlantic and Gulf coasts. Dungeness crab is caught on the Pacific coast. King crab and snow crab come from frigid waters of the North Pacific, stone crab from semi-tropical waters off Florida, and Jonah and red crab off the north Atlantic coast.

Blue crab is easily recognized by its blue claws and oval, dark-blue to brownish shells mottled with blue and cream. Blue crab is marketed in both hard- and soft-shell stages.

From spring through fall, most blue crab have hard shells. They range in size from 1/4 to 1 pound. Hard-shell crab are sold live or cooked whole, or as frozen, canned or pasteurized crabmeat. The choicest crabmeat is *lump meat* or *backfin,* which consists of whole pieces of white meat from the body. It is used in recipes when appearance is important. *Flaked meat* is small pieces from the body and *claw meat* is picked from the claws. Claw meat is dark and delicious. Pasteurized crabmeat is heated in cans to a temperature lower than that used in canning, but high enough to kill most bacteria. It can be stored up to six months unopened in the refrigerator. Once

opened, it must be used within three to five days.

Unless they will be sautéed or stewed, clean and crack hard-shell blue crabs after they're cooked. *To clean and crack crab before cooking,* immerse in boiling water two to three minutes to kill but not cook them. Drain and rinse under cold water. Clean and crack the crab as shown above, but leave the legs attached.

Soft-shell crabs are molting blue crabs that have shed their hard shells to grow larger ones. The soft-shell season runs from mid-April through mid-September, peaking in June and July. Considered a delicacy, soft-shell crabs are usually sautéed, broiled or deep-fried, and the whole crab, including the soft outer layer, is eaten. Soft-shell crabs range from two to five ounces each. Two or three crabs make a meal. *To dress soft-shell blue crabs,* see page 82.

To use blue crab and Dungeness crab in preparing dishes, simmer in salted water or Court Bouillon, page 34, 10 to 20 minutes. Plunge into cold water to cool and prevent overcooking. Drain well, then extract the meat.

Dungeness Crab—Ranging in size from 1-1/4 to 3-1/2 pounds, Dungeness crab comes to market live, cooked whole, frozen whole or in sections, or canned as crabmeat.

Steaming or boiling is the simplest and most popular way to cook live crab. It can also be grilled, sautéed or stir-fried.

Dungeness crab may be cleaned and cracked before or after cooking. It is necessary to kill, then clean and crack the crab before using the meat in stews, or when grilling, sautéing or stir-frying. Clean and crack crab after cooking when they have been boiled or steamed.

To kill Dungeness crab before cooking, grasp the live crab from the rear, firmly holding the last two legs on each side. Place the crab upside down on a cutting board. In this position, it is helpless. Place a heavy, sharp knife, cutting-edge down, along its midsection between the legs. Hit the knife a hard, quick blow with a mallet or hammer. This will kill the crab instantly. If you would rather kill it by immersing in boiling water two to three minutes. Then rinse under cold running water. However, boiling may dilute the flavor and cook some of the meat. If desired, have your retailer dress the crab for you, or follow these directions:

To clean and crack raw or cooked Dungeness crab, after killing the crab, remove the top or back shell. See photos at left. Hold the base of the crab with one hand; place the thumb under the shell at midpoint and pull firmly. Shell will come off easily. Cut off the face. Pull out and discard the bile sac. Turn the crab on its back; lift up and pull off the *apron,* which is a rough triangle of shell. Pull out and discard the gray feathery gills. Save the creamy crab fat, also called *butter.* Mix it with melted butter for a delicious dip. Rinse out the top shell and the center of the crab, removing the small white intestine. If the crab is to be left intact, crack the leg and claw sections with a mallet or hammer, leaving the legs attached.

To cut up a Dungeness crab, twist off the claws and legs where they join the body. Crack each section of the claws and legs with a mallet or hammer, being careful not to crush the meat. Cut the body into several pieces for easy removal. Pick over the meat to remove any cartilage. Rinse raw-crab pieces thoroughly.

King Crab—This large crab averages 10 pounds, with a leg span of about 4 feet. The dwindling catch is rigidly controlled by quotas to protect future supplies, but this causes higher prices. King crab is recognized by its snow-white meat edged in bright red. A small amount is marketed fresh, but most king crab is cooked and sold as frozen legs, claws and *clusters.* Clusters are shoulder sections with several legs attached. These clusters may be whole in-shell, split for easy removal of meat from the shell, or shelled.

Snow Crab—Although half the size of king crab, snow crab is still larger than most. Known for its sweet, delicate flavor and tender texture, it is considered to have a superior flavor and texture to king crab. Snow crab is sold as frozen clusters and claws, and as crabmeat.

Stone Crab—Nearly all of the edible meat of stone crab is in the claws. It is characterized by a hard, dense shell and large claws with black tips. The claws are often removed and cooked immediately after trapping. They are then chilled or frozen. Because stone-crab claws are so hard, the first and second knuckle are usually cracked so the meat can be removed easily.

Crayfish

Crayfish is better known in some places as *crawfish* or *crawdads.* These small freshwater crustaceans are found in rivers and estuaries—where a river and the sea meet. Louisiana is the biggest producing region in the United States—almost 20 million pounds a year—but many other places in the world harvest substantial numbers. Crawfish range in size from two to eight ounces. Like shrimp, most of the meat is in the tail. See Spicy Boiled Crayfish, page 44.

Langostinos

This crustacean is caught in the Gulf of Mexico and off the coast of South America. Sometimes marketed as *rock shrimp,* its flavor is a cross between shrimp and lobster. It is commonly used in salads and soups, or as you would use cooked lobster. Langostinos are generally sold cooked and frozen.

Lobster

As late as the 1880s, lobster was so common it was used for fish bait. Those days are past. Due to the overwhelming demand for this *king of shellfish,* lobster harvesting has declined significantly and the price of lobster keeps rising.

Two kinds of lobster are commonly available. The best known is American lobster, also called *Maine lobster.* Maine lobster are most abundant in the cold waters off Maine, Newfoundland and Nova Scotia. Generally, the colder the water, the tastier and more succulent the flesh, which is why Maine lobster is so highly prized.

Maine lobster average one to five pounds in weight. Their greenish-blue to reddish-brown color turns bright red when cooked. They may be purchased live, cooked whole, frozen whole, frozen tails and as canned meat.

Spiny lobster, also known as *rock lobster,* are caught in waters off Australia, Florida, Mexico, New Zealand, South Africa and Southern California. They do not have large heavy claws, so most of the meat is in the tail. Spiny lobster are marketed primarily as uncooked frozen tails.

Purchasing & Preparing Lobster—Fish retailers keep lobster alive in holding tanks. Claws are kept closed by pins or elastic bands because lobster are cannibalistic and will destroy each other. The more active lobster are the most recently caught. Keep live lobster in the refrigerator up to 12 hours. Do not put them in fresh water. Lobster will not make you ill if they die before they're cooked, but cooking should not be delayed. As it ages, the tail shrinks to less than half the original size and the meat becomes mushy and unpalatable.

If you buy preboiled lobster in-the-shell, the tail should be pulled in tightly under the body. This means the lobster was alive when cooked.

Lobster may be cleaned before or after cooking. Live lobster may be boiled, steamed, broiled, grilled or baked. When it will be broiled and grilled, lobster must be killed before it is cleaned.

To clean and prepare live Maine lobster for broiling and grilling, place the lobster, stomach-side down, on a work surface. Plunge the tip of a sharp knife into the lobster at the point where the tail and body join. This will sever the spinal cord and kill the lobster instantly. If it still moves, it is purely muscle reflex. Cut off the legs. Turn the lobster over and draw the knife down through the undershell and flesh. If the lobster is larger than 1 to 1-1/2 pounds, cut in half lengthwise through the back shell. If it is less than 1-1/2 pounds, so that you're serving 1 lobster per person, cut through the undershell and flesh. Then, using both hands, press the lobster open so it lies flat to expose the flesh evenly to heat. Remove the small stomach sac near the eyes. Pull out the intestinal vein running down the tail. Save the *roe,* or eggs, if there are any, and the greenish liver, called *tomalley.* The roe and tomalley are considered delicacies. Crack the claws and large leg joints with a mallet or hammer.

To clean and crack cooked lobster for salads, hors d'oeuvres and sauced dishes, boil or steam the lobster, page 46. This kills it instantly. Plunge the cooked lobster into cold water to cool and prevent

How to Clean & Crack Whole Cooked Lobster

1/Twist off tail. With lobster on its back, cut in half. Remove stomach sac, eyes and intestinal vein.

2/Break off claws. Use a lobster cracker to crack lobster and crab claws. A nutcracker may be substituted.

overcooking. Twist off the tail. Remove the meat from the tail by cutting through the soft membrane on both sides of the undershell with kitchen shears, page 93. Lift out the meat in one piece. With the lobster on its back, cut in half. Remove the stomach sac, eyes and intestinal vein. Save the roe and tomalley. Break off the claws and remove the meat. Break off the small legs and extract the meat with a small fork or a pick. See photos on opposite page.

To use frozen spiny-lobster tails, thaw frozen tails in the refrigerator before cooking. If you can purchase live spiny lobster, boil or steam them, then clean as directed above. If you prefer to broil or grill spiny lobster, they're easier to handle if boiled or steamed first. Then split in half, clean and broil long enough to reheat.

Mussels

Mussels are one of the lowest priced and most under-utilized shellfish in North America. They are found in abundance off the Atlantic and Pacific coasts.

Most mussels are harvested wild, but increasing numbers are being farmed. New Zealand mussels are fairly new on the world market. They have delicate green shells and sweet, succulent meat. They are raised on ropes, which keeps them off the silty sea bottom and makes them clean and sand-free. They are almost twice the size of other mussels.

Atlantic mussels are the most common. Their bluish to jet-black shells are 2-1/2 to 3 inches long. They are larger than sweet, tender California mussels, averaging 12 per pound and 20 per pound respectively. The best time to purchase fresh mussels is from October to April. In the late spring and early summer, mussels spawn and are lean and watery, but still edible. However, from May 1 to October 31, California mussels are under strict quarantine for paralytic shellfish poisoning (PSP) toxin that may be present.

Mussels are available live in-the-shell, frozen, canned and smoked. Live mussels have their shells closed or will close their shells when tapped or pressed. Refrigerate them, covered with a damp towel. Do not put them in fresh water.

Mussels anchor themselves to rocks and pilings along the beach with a bundle of tough fibers called *byssus, threads* or *beards.* Some mussels are sold de-bearded, but they die soon after the beards are removed. To keep them more than a day, buy them with beards on.

Most mussels sold commercially have been cleaned, graded by size, and purged of sand and mud. If you collect mussels yourself, purge them as directed for clams, page 23, and scrub the barnacles and residue from the shells. De-beard them by grasping the beard and removing it with a tug, page 109.

Unlike oysters and clams, mussels are not usually eaten raw, but are generally steamed, simmered or stewed. One of the simplest and best ways to prepare them is *marinière* or sailor-style, page 41.

Oysters

Despite Jonathan Swift's declaration, *"He was a bold man that first ate an oyster,"* about 90 million pounds of these mollusks are eaten each year. Natural oyster beds are found off the Atlantic, Pacific and Gulf coasts. Today, about half of the oysters marketed are farmed. There are three primary species harvested on a commercial basis. These include Eastern or Atlantic, Pacific and Olympia oysters. Within these species are numerous varieties that vary considerably in flavor and texture, depending on where they're harvested.

Eastern or Atlantic oysters are taken from waters along the Atlantic seaboard. The name usually indicates where the oyster was grown, such as *Blue Point, Cape Cod, Long Island, Chincoteague, Cotuit* and *Apalachicola.*

Pacific oysters were originally transplanted from Japan. Now they inhabit much of the Pacific coastline. Like Eastern oysters, they're sold under several names, indicating where they're grown.

Olympia oysters are native to Pacific waters. They have been over-harvested and today are found only in Washington's Puget Sound. Olympia oysters are prized for their delicate flavor and small size.

European Belon oyster is regarded as one of the finest tasting oysters available. It is now being farmed in the United States.

Oysters are marketed as live in-the-shell, fresh or frozen shucked meat, canned and smoked. Oysters have a shallow and a deep-cup shell. Refrigerate live oysters with their deep-cup shell down so the juice, or *liquor,* won't leak out. Cover them with a damp towel, but do not cover them with fresh water. This will kill them. Discard any oysters that are open, bad-smelling or dried out when you open them. Shucked oysters should be plump, have a natural creamy color, fresh aroma and clear liquor surrounding them.

The saying that oysters should not be eaten in

How to Shuck Oysters

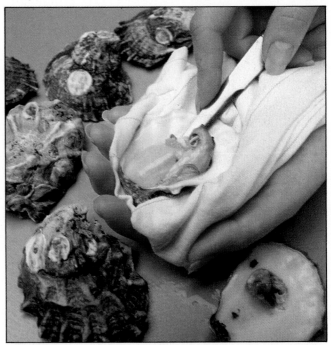

1/Use a towel to protect your hand. With deep-cup shell down, push tip of an oyster knife or punch-type can opener between shell halves near hinge.

2/Slide knife around top shell to sever muscle holding shell halves together. Slide knife or your thumb under oyster to sever bottom muscle.

months without an **R** is a myth. Good oysters are available year-round. However, they're at their best for serving on-the-half-shell during the fall and winter.

Some oyster-lovers believe that there's only one way to eat an oyster—raw on-the-half-shell with a squeeze of lemon juice and a few grains of pepper. Oysters can be cooked by a variety of methods. Regardless of the cooking method, be sure to remove them from the heat when their edges start to curl. Overcooked oysters have the texture of leather.

Shucking oysters is a skill that demands practice. Most fish dealers will shuck them for you, but oyster connoisseurs think that to enjoy a raw oyster's full flavor, it should be consumed within 5 minutes of shucking. An oyster knife, page 31, with its short, broad blade, makes quick and easy work of shucking oysters. A punch-type can opener makes opening the oyster easy, but a knife must be used to cut the oyster loose from the shell.

To shuck an oyster, scrub the shell thoroughly. If you cut your hand while shucking an oyster, it can become badly infected.

Therefore, use a folded towel or potholder to protect your hand. Place the oyster, deep-cup-side down, on a flat surface. Push the tip of the oyster knife or punch-type can opener between the shell-halves near the hinge. Pry upward. This should release the shell. Slide the knife around the top shell to sever the muscle holding the shells together. Be careful not to puncture the oyster. Remove and discard the top shell. Slide the knife or your thumb under the oyster to sever the bottom muscle. For **oysters on-the-half-shell,** serve the raw oyster and liquor in the bottom shell.

Scallops

The name *scallop* aptly describes the fluted edge of this mollusk's fan-shape shell. Its tender, delicate and slightly sweet meat should be cooked very briefly.

Scallops are caught off the Atlantic coast. Unlike other *bivalves,* scallops can't hold their shells tightly closed. They die soon after they're taken from the water. Because of their perishability, scallops are usually shucked, trimmed and iced aboard fishing boats as soon as they're caught. In Europe, the entire scallop, including the mass that surrounds the muscle and the female's crescent-shape coral-colored roe, is eaten. In North America, roe is usually trimmed off, although many fish markets are selling imported scallops with the roe attached.

Of the more than 400 species of scallops, three are most common. *Sea scallop* is large and flavorful. *Bay scallop,* which is tiny, more delicate and more tender than the sea scallop, is less plentiful and more expensive. *Calico scallop* is a relatively new commercial species from the Gulf of Mexico and the east coast of Florida. It is slightly larger than the bay scallop and gets its name from the mottled or calico appearance of the shell.

Scallops are sold fresh and frozen. Their color varies from cream to tan to light orange, depending on their diet. *Snow-white scallops should be avoided*—they have been soaked in water to increase their weight and improve appearance, but soaking compromises flavor. Fresh scallops smell mild and sweet, and have a gleaming, moist appearance.

Shrimp

To many people, seafood and shrimp are synonymous. There are hundreds of saltwater and freshwater species of shrimp throughout the world. When purchased, fresh shrimp should have a mild aroma and firm flesh.

Because there is virtually no meat on the head section of shrimp, the heads are usually removed aboard fishing boats. Shrimp are classified by size according to the number of shrimp per pound. For example, jumbo shrimp average 16 to 25 per pound; tiny ocean shrimp yield more than 70 per pound. The weight of medium and large shrimp come between these. Tiny ocean shrimp, in some areas called *bay shrimp,* are almost always sold shelled and cooked. One pound of raw shrimp yields 1/2 to 3/4 pound cooked shelled meat.

Shrimp is available raw or cooked, peeled or unpeeled, fresh or frozen. The terms *shrimp* and *prawn* are used interchangeably, with prawn usually referring to larger shrimp. *Scampi* is a term used by some retailers when referring to larger shrimp. Actually, scampi is the name of a recipe.

Connoisseurs believe that shrimp cooked in the shell have more flavor than shrimp shelled before cooking. This is a matter of personal preference and depends on the way the shrimp will be used. Another matter of preference is whether or not to devein shrimp. The black in-

testinal vein, or *sand vein,* runs down the back of shrimp just under the surface of the flesh. In many cases, leaving the vein will not affect the shrimp's flavor. It is removed primarily for aesthetic reasons. In larger shrimp, the vein may be sandy or gritty and should be removed.

Shell shrimp within 20 minutes of cooking to keep the shell from becoming brittle and hard to remove. Remove the legs and open the shell lengthwise. Gently pull the shell back, starting at the head end. Leave the tail *feathers* attached, if desired. The tail is decorative and convenient to grasp when cooking or eating.

Devein shrimp raw or cooked, before or after shelling. For quick deveining, make a shallow cut lengthwise down the back of each shrimp. Rinse out the vein. If you don't want the shrimp to show a cut down the back, insert a slender sharp skewer or wooden pick beneath the vein. Grasp the end of the vein and carefully pull it out.

How to Devein Shrimp

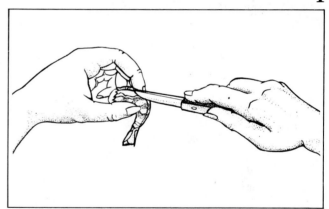

Cut down center back; remove vein.

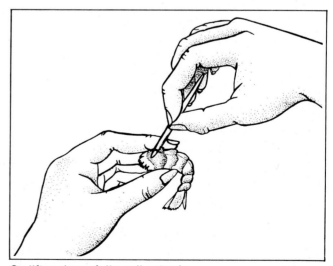

Or, lift and carefully pull out vein.

How to Clean Squid

1/Pull gently to separate tentacles, viscera and ink sac from body. Pull out transparent sword-shape pen from body.

2/Cut off tentacles above eyes. Reserve tentacles. Squeeze the hard, round beak from base of tentacles. Discard beak.

Squid

Squid has earned the title of *poor-man's abalone,* and for good reason. This shellfish has a firm, mild, sweet flesh similar to that of abalone, yet at a fraction of the cost.

Squid, also called *calamari* and *inkfish,* is available fresh and frozen. Fresh squid has a fresh, mildly sweet aroma and ivory-colored flesh beneath its speckled transparent covering. Any yellowing of the flesh is a sign the squid is old.

For tender, succulent squid, cook it no more than 3 minutes, unless stewing; then cook no less than 20 minutes. Otherwise, the squid will be tough and chewy. Squid must be cleaned before cooking. Once cleaned, the entire body and tentacles are edible.

To clean a squid, hold the body in one hand and the base of the tentacles just above the eyes in the other hand. Pull gently to separate the body and tentacles. Pull out the transparent sword-shape pen from the body. Pull out and discard the viscera and ink sac. Rinse the body cavity. Trim the wings, if desired.

Cut off the tentacles just above the eyes; discard the eyes, but save the tentacles. Squeeze the small hard, round beak—that looks like a garbanzo bean—from the base of the tentacles. Discard the beak. Pull off and discard the transparent, speckled membrane covering large squid. The membrane of small squid is tender and adds color to a dish.

Equipment & Tools

Many tools needed for working with fish and shellfish are standard in today's kitchens. Specialized cookware, such as a fish poacher or hinged wire basket, will make preparation of some recipes easier. The following tools and cookware are useful:

- **Basket, Hinged Wire**—The oval, open-mesh basket can be placed on a grill or the legs can be extended, letting you place the fish directly over the coals as illustrated on page 91.
- **Cracker, Lobster**—This nutcracker-shape instrument is useful for cracking lobster and crab claws. A nutcracker may be substituted.
- **Brush, Stiff-Bristle**—A brush that fits comfortably in your hand is useful for scrubbing mussels, clams and oysters.
- **Knife, Clam**—A clam knife has a short blade with a blunt tip to avoid cutting the clam meat. Another clam opener has a pocket to hold the clam and a short-blade knife that is forced between the clam shells, page 23. A small paring knife may be substituted.
- **Knife, Filleting**—A filleting knife is essential for boning and filleting fish. Its tapered 7- to 9-inch blade must be thin and flexible enough to slide over the bones as you slice off the fillets. You can also use a sharp, thin slicing knife or boning knife.
- **Knife, Oyster**—The short, sturdy blade of an oyster knife is sometimes shaped like an arrowhead. A punch-type can opener can be used to open the oyster, but a knife is needed to cut the muscle loose from the shell, page 28.
- **Mallet, Wooden or Rubber**—This handy tool is useful for cracking crab shells or to add force to a knife when cutting through shells or bones.
- **Poacher**—A fish poacher is an oblong pan, about 6 inches deep, with a tight-fitting lid. The rack in some poachers can be raised, making it possible to steam fish. Poachers range from 10 to 36 inches in length. Larger poachers are used over two stovetop burners.
- **Scaler**—There are several types of these saw-toothed implements used to scrape scales off fish, page 10. A dull paring knife can be substituted when scaling small fish.
- **Shears, Kitchen**—Heavy-duty kitchen shears or fish shears make it easy to trim fins and tails. Shears can also be used for cutting rib bones.
- **Steamer**—Many types of steamers are available, from the stacked Oriental bamboo steamer designed to fit in or on a wok, to pots fitted with a steamer basket. You can improvise a steamer by using a deep pot or roaster with a tight-fitting lid. Place a wire rack and empty tuna cans, with tops and bottoms removed, inside the pot or roaster.
- **Tweezers or Needle-Nose Pliers**—These are helpful for removing stubborn or hard-to-reach bones.

Farming Fish & Shellfish

Supplies of fish were once thought to be limitless, but over-fishing, pollution and changing environments have caused a short supply. *Aquaculture,* the practice of raising and breeding fish and shellfish in a controlled environment, is becoming more and more important to supplying markets with seafood. Aquaculture includes a variety of techniques, from the simple protection and maintenance of oyster beds to creating total artificial environments. Each technique shares the common goal of increasing the food yield per acre of water. Today, all of the rainbow trout and much of the catfish and oysters sold in the United States and Canada are farmed. Projects are underway for raising salmon, lobster, mussels and many other species of fish and shellfish.

Poaching, Steaming & Steeping

Poaching, steaming and steeping keep fish and shellfish moist and tender. They also eliminate the need for cooking fat—a boon to the calorie-conscious.

Firm-texture fish, such as trout, salmon and striped bass, hold their shape well when poached, steamed or steeped. High-fat and soft-texture fish, such as sablefish, herring and bluefish, usually fall apart when cooked in liquid.

Poaching is the term used for cooking food in liquid that *quivers* but does not bubble. Bundles of Sole are gently simmered in a flavorful liquid. Beer-Boiled Shrimp are poached in a simmering beer mixture. The liquid never actually boils.

To poach, use an oblong fish poacher or a wide shallow pan, such as a skillet, heavy saucepan or pot. When poaching large whole fish, an oblong fish poacher fitted with a perforated rack is ideal. Or, use a roasting pan or large kettle. Wrap the fish in cheesecloth, leaving long ends to lift the fish in and out of the liquid.

Poaching liquid may be lightly salted water, milk, fish stock or Court Bouillon, which is a combination of water and wine seasoned with vegetables and herbs. Wine is an acid and keeps the fish firm and white. Poaching liquid may be strained and reused, or reduced to make a sauce.

Steamed fish and shellfish are cooked *over* boiling liquid, not in it. Steam provides a gentle, even heat that preserves the natural juices and delicate texture of fish. The liquid used for steaming may be plain water, or water seasoned with herbs, spices and wine. Chinese Steamed Whole Fish is seasoned with onions, gingerroot and sesame oil. Flavor is superb and the fish is tender and moist.

A steam-cooker is ideal for steaming, but any deep pan with a tight-fitting lid is satisfactory. Improvise by setting a perforated tray or wire rack on empty tuna cans inside the pan, as discussed on page 31.

Steeping is similar to poaching. Unlike poaching, which uses direct heat to keep the cooking liquid at a simmer, steeping uses only the warmth of the hot liquid. Because there is no agitation, the delicate texture and appearance of fish are preserved. It is an excellent way to cook individual fish fillets, steaks, small whole fish and shellfish, such as shrimp and shucked oysters.

Flavor the steeping liquid any way you desire. In Steeped Fish, the steeping liquid contains lemon slices, onion, parsley or dried thyme, salt and pepper. After the liquid comes to a full boil, remove the pan from the heat. Gently lower fish into the hot liquid, then cover the pan tightly. Steep until the fish is done; time depends on its weight and thickness.

Steamed Monkfish with Vegetable Sauce

Vegetables cook in the bottom of the steamer as the fish cooks on top.

1/2 lb. leeks
1/2 cup water
3/4 cup dry white wine
1 tablespoon butter or margarine
1-1/2 lbs. monkfish or
  other angler fillets
Salt
White pepper

1 medium carrot,
  cut in julienne strips
1 small tomato, peeled,
  seeded, chopped
1/3 cup whipping cream
1/4 cup butter or margarine,
  room temperature
Finely chopped parsley

Cut white part of leeks into julienne strips; discard green tops. Place julienned leeks, water, wine and 1 tablespoon butter or margarine in bottom of a steamer. Cover; simmer about 8 minutes. Rinse fillets; cut into 4 or 5 servings. Lightly season each serving with salt and white pepper. Add carrots to bottom of steamer. Place seasoned fish on top rack of steamer. Cover; steam 6 to 8 minutes or until fish tests done. Place cooked fish on a platter; cover loosely with foil to keep warm. Add tomato to leek mixture. Stirring occasionally, simmer until heated through. Using a slotted spoon, place cooked vegetables in a serving dish; keep warm. Bring cooking liquid to a boil. Boil rapidly until reduced to 2 tablespoons. Stir in cream and fish juices that have collected on platter. Cook until reduced by one-half. Reduce heat to very low. Whisk in 1/4 cup butter or margarine, a little at a time, until sauce becomes thick and creamy. Add salt and white pepper to taste. Stir cooked vegetables into sauce. Spoon sauce and vegetables over fish. Garnish with chopped parsley. Makes 4 or 5 servings.

An acid, such as lemon juice, wine or vinegar, added to the liquid for poaching, steeping or steaming fish, keeps the flesh firmer and whiter.

Bundles of Sole

Beautiful and elegant!

4 to 6 cups Court Bouillon, below
18 to 24 slender asparagus spears
2 green onions
6 (4- to 6-oz.) skinless sole,
   flounder or pompano fillets

Salt
White pepper
Sauce Mousseline, page 154,
   or Beurre Blanc, page 146

Prepare Court Bouillon. Meanwhile, trim asparagus into even lengths; peel stalks, if desired. Use 24 asparagus spears if spears are very thin. In a large 2-inch-deep skillet, cook asparagus in boiling Court Bouillon until tender. Use a slotted spoon or tongs to remove asparagus. Quickly plunge into ice water; drain on paper towels. Reserve liquid in skillet; bring to a simmer. Cut long green shoots from onions. Add green shoots to simmering liquid. Simmer 3 to 4 minutes or until tender. Use a slotted spoon or tongs to remove onion shoots from cooking liquid. Quickly plunge into ice water; drain on paper towels. Reserve cooking liquid. Gently rinse sole; pat dry with paper towels. Season with salt and white pepper. Lay fish on a flat surface, skinned- or dark-side down. Lay 3 or 4 cooked asparagus spears crosswise on each fillet. Roll up fillets from a narrow end. Tie rolls with blanched green-onion shoots. Refrigerate up to 8 hours or continue with preparation. *Do not refrigerate overnight.* Prepare Sauce Mousseline or Beurre Blanc. Set over warm, *not simmering,* water to keep warm. In a large skillet, bring Court Bouillon to a simmer. Carefully lower fish bundles into bouillon. Bouillon does not need to completely cover bundles. Gently simmer 5 to 8 minutes or until fish tests done. Turn once with a spatula or tongs during cooking. Using a slotted spoon, carefully remove cooked bundles from bouillon; drain on paper towels. Serve with Sauce Mousseline or Beurre Blanc. Makes 6 servings.

Variation

Sole bundles may be steamed over boiling water rather than poached. Steam 5 to 8 minutes or until fish tests done.

Court Bouillon

A seasoned liquid used for poaching fish.

1 qt. water
1 qt. dry white wine
5 or 6 black peppercorns
1 medium onion, thinly sliced
1 large leek, thinly sliced,
   or another medium onion
1 large carrot, thinly sliced

1 celery stalk, thinly sliced
8 parsley sprigs
2 thyme sprigs or
   1/2 teaspoon dried leaf thyme,
   crumbled
1 bay leaf
About 1 teaspoon salt

Combine all ingredients in a large kettle. Bring to a boil. Reduce heat; simmer 30 minutes. Place a strainer over a large bowl; line with a double thickness of cheesecloth. Pour liquid through cheesecloth. Discard vegetables and herbs. Makes 6 cups.

Variation

Add 1/2 teaspoon fennel seeds.

Sole & Scallop Quenelles

Use your food processor or blender for easy preparation of these savory quenelles.

6 cups Fish Stock, page 101,
   Court Bouillon, page 34, or water
1/2 lb. sole, pike, whiting or other lean,
   white, skinless fish fillets
1/2 lb. scallops
2 eggs, separated
1/4 cup butter or margarine,
   room temperature

1/2 cup whipping cream
3/4 to 1 teaspoon salt
1/4 teaspoon white pepper
1/4 teaspoon ground nutmeg
Tomato-Cream Sauce, see below
Chopped chives

Tomato-Cream Sauce:
1 tablespoon butter or margarine
1/2 small onion, finely chopped
3 small tomatoes, peeled, seeded, chopped
Pinch of sugar

Salt and pepper
2 tablespoons dry white wine or vermouth
1/2 cup whipping cream

Prepare Fish Stock or Court Bouillon. Cut fish into 2-inch chunks. In a food processor fitted with a metal blade, puree fish and scallops using quick on and off pulses until mixture is smooth. Or, grind fish and scallops twice in a food grinder, using fine blade. Then puree in a blender. Process one-third at a time, if necessary. Add egg yolks and butter or margarine; process to a fine paste. Add egg whites; process until blended. Add cream, salt, white pepper and nutmeg. Process until smooth and creamy. Spoon mixture into a large bowl; cover and refrigerate 3 to 4 hours. When ready to make quenelles, prepare Tomato-Cream Sauce. In a deep skillet or large saucepan, bring Fish Stock, Court Bouillon or water to a simmer. Preheat oven to 165F (75C). *To cook quenelles,* dip 2 soup or dessert spoons into hot water. Use 1 hot, wet spoon to scoop an oval mound of chilled mixture. Smooth top with second hot, wet spoon. Using both spoons, loosen quenelle; carefully lower into simmering liquid. Wet spoons each time before making another quenelle. Do not crowd quenelles in pan. Gently simmer 6 to 8 minutes or until quenelles are firm and float to surface. Use a slotted spoon to remove cooked quenelles from hot liquid; drain on paper towels. Place drained quenelles in a medium serving bowl; keep warm in oven until all are cooked. Spoon Tomato-Cream Sauce over top. Sprinkle with chopped chives. Makes 25 to 30 quenelles.

Tomato-Cream Sauce:
Melt butter or margarine in a medium skillet or saucepan. Add onion; sauté until soft and transparent. Add tomatoes and sugar. Add salt and pepper to taste. Cook over medium-high heat until most of liquid evaporates. In a food processor or blender, process tomato mixture and wine or vermouth until smooth. Or, press tomato mixture through a food mill or fine sieve; stir in wine or vermouth. Return to skillet or saucepan. Gradually stir in cream. Bring to a simmer; do not boil. Adjust seasonings to taste. Makes 1-1/4 cups.

Add onion, celery, garlic and herbs to steaming water. The flavors are carried by the steam to the fish. For even flavoring and cooking, the steam must circulate freely inside the steamer.

How to Make Sole & Scallop Quenelles

1/Puree sole and scallops in blender or food processor. Add other ingredients as directed.

2/Use hot, wet spoons to scoop an oval mound of chilled mixture. Cook mounds in simmering liquid until firm.

Smoky Poached Fish

Liquid smoke added to the poaching liquid gives the fish a faint smoky flavor.

6 cups water
3 tablespoons natural-hickory liquid smoke
1/2 small onion, sliced
1 celery stalk, sliced
4 or 5 parsley sprigs

4 (4- to 8-oz.) lean fish steaks,
  chunks or skinless fillets
4 lemon wedges
Parsley sprigs, if desired

In a deep skillet or pan large enough to hold fish in a single layer, combine water, liquid smoke, onion, celery and 4 or 5 parsley sprigs. Bring liquid to a boil; add fish. Liquid should completely cover fish. If it does not, add boiling water and liquid smoke using a ratio of 1 cup water to 1-1/2 teaspoons liquid smoke. Reduce heat until liquid gently simmers. Cook until fish tests done. Remove fish from liquid; drain on paper towels. Serve immediately or refrigerate fish 1 hour or until chilled. To serve immediately, arrange drained fish on a platter. Garnish with lemon wedges and parsley, if desired. Flake cold fish; use in salads or sandwiches. Makes 4 servings.

Chinese Steamed Whole Fish

Steaming preserves the natural juices and fresh flavor of fish.

3 green onions
1 (2-1/2- to 3-lb.) rockfish,
   red snapper, tilefish,
   grouper or sea bass, cleaned, scaled
Salt
2 tablespoons sesame oil

4 slices gingerroot,
   cut in 1/16-inch-thick julienne strips
1 or 2 green onions
1/4 cup peanut oil
8 to 10 cilantro sprigs
2 tablespoons soy sauce

Lay 3 green onions on a flat surface; use flat side of a knife blade to crush onions. Place 2 crushed onions lengthwise on a heatproof dish or platter that will fit inside a steamer or roasting pan. Rinse fish; pat dry inside and out with paper towels. Season lightly inside and out with salt. Place seasoned fish on crushed onions on platter. Drizzle 1 tablespoon sesame oil over fish. Spread half of gingerroot over fish. Lay remaining crushed onion lengthwise on fish. Place dish or platter on a rack in a steamer or roaster. Cover; steam over simmering water 10 to 15 minutes or until fish tests done. Meanwhile, slice remaining green onions into 2-1/2- to 3-inch slivers. In a small saucepan, slowly heat peanut oil with remaining 1 tablespoon sesame oil until hot but not smoking. When fish is done, lift dish or platter from steamer or roaster. Discard liquid that has accumulated in dish. Discard cooked green onions and gingerroot. Place steamed fish on a platter. Sprinkle remaining gingerroot, green-onion slivers, 4 or 5 cilantro sprigs and soy sauce on fish. Spoon on hot oil mixture; oil mixture will sizzle. Garnish with remaining cilantro sprigs, if desired. To serve, cut down center back of cooked fish to backbone. Using a knife, separate upper fillet from backbone. Cut upper fillet into serving pieces. Slide a wide metal spatula between flesh and ribs. Lift off each serving with toppings; place on individual plates or on a platter. When top fillet has been removed, remove backbone; serve remaining fish. Makes 4 to 5 servings.

Sherry-Sauced Fillets

Frozen fish fillets are poached to perfection in a sherried tomato sauce.

2 (1-lb.) pkgs. frozen skinless
   fish fillets
Salt and pepper
2 to 3 tablespoons olive oil or
   vegetable oil
1 small onion, chopped
2 garlic cloves, minced

1 (16-oz.) can stewed tomatoes,
   drained, coarsely chopped
2 tablespoons tomato paste
3 tablespoons chopped parsley
4 to 6 tablespoons dry sherry
1/4 teaspoon sugar

Let fish stand at room temperature 20 minutes; do not thaw completely. Cut each 1-pound block into 3 portions. Season lightly with salt and pepper. Heat oil in a skillet with a tight-fitting lid, large enough to hold fish in a single layer. Add onion and garlic; sauté over medium heat until onion is soft and transparent. Add tomatoes, tomato paste, parsley, sherry and sugar. Add salt and pepper to taste. Add fish to skillet, spooning sauce over fish. Cover and gently simmer 18 to 20 minutes or until fish tests done. Serve immediately. Makes 6 servings.

How to Make Chinese Steamed Whole Fish

1/Cut down center back of cooked fish to backbone. Using a knife, separate upper fillet from backbone.

2/After top fillet has been removed, lift out backbone; serve remaining fish.

Teriyaki Fish

You'll get a taste of the Orient with this succulent fish.

1-1/4 to 1-1/2 lbs. lean skinless
   fish fillets or 4 fish steaks
1/4 cup bottled teriyaki sauce

2 tablespoons lemon or lime juice
2 tablespoons butter or margarine

Toppings:
Chopped green onions
Toasted sesame seeds

Chopped dry-roasted peanuts
Chopped cilantro or parsley

Rinse fish; pat dry with paper towels. Cut fillets into 4 equal portions. In a shallow bowl, combine teriyaki sauce and lemon or lime juice. Add fish; marinate in refrigerator or at room temperature 15 minutes. Drain fish, reserving marinade. Melt butter or margarine in a large skillet with a cover. Add fish; sauté quickly over medium-high heat, no more than 30 seconds on each side. Add reserved marinade. Cover pan; reduce heat. Gently simmer 3 to 5 minutes until fish tests done. Arrange cooked fish on a platter. Sprinkle with 1 or more toppings; serve immediately. Makes 4 servings.

Steeped Fish

Fish cooked by this gentle method will be moist and smooth-textured.

**1/3 lb. to 2 lbs. fish steaks,
   skinless fillets, fish chunks or
   small fish, cleaned, scaled**
Water
2 lemon slices
**1 green onion, sliced,
   or 1 slice yellow onion**

**4 or 5 parsley sprigs or
   other fresh herbs,
   or 3/4 teaspoon dried leaf thyme**
1/2 teaspoon salt
1/8 teaspoon pepper

Rinse fish. Place rinsed fish in a fish poacher or large shallow pan. Add enough water to cover fish by 1 inch. Lift fish from water; set aside. To water, add lemon slices, onion, parsley or fresh or dried herbs, salt and pepper. Cover and bring to a full boil. Remove pan from heat. Gently lower fish into hot liquid. Immediately cover pan tightly. Steep 3 to 10 minutes, depending on weight and thickness of fish. *To serve hot,* drain and serve immediately. *To serve cold,* lift fish from pan and plunge into ice water to cool quickly. Drain on paper towels. Makes 1 to 6 servings.

Variations

Substitute Court Bouillon, page 34, or Fish Stock, page 101, for water, lemon, onion and seasonings.

Substitute 1 to 1-1/2 pounds shrimp for fish. Shell and devein shrimp before or after steeping.

Poached Finnan Haddie

Superb for breakfast with scrambled eggs and toast.

**Velouté Sauce, page 147,
   or Dill Butter, page 156**
2 lbs. finnan haddie

Equal amounts of milk and water
Lemon wedges

Prepare Velouté Sauce or Dill Butter; set aside. Rinse fish; taste a small piece. If it is very salty, soak haddie in water to cover 30 minutes. Place rinsed or soaked fish in a large skillet. Add equal amounts of milk and water, adding enough liquid to cover fish. Remove fish; bring liquid to a simmer. Return fish to skillet. Cover; poach fish in simmering liquid 8 to 12 minutes or until fish tests done. Remove fish from poaching liquid; drain. Serve with Velouté Sauce or Dill Butter and lemon wedges. Makes 4 servings.

Poached, steamed and steeped fish are cooked without fat and therefore are lower in calorie than fish cooked by other methods.

Moules Marinière

Serve bowls of steamy mussels with crusty French bread.

4 to 5 dozen mussels
3 tablespoons butter or margarine
1/4 cup finely chopped shallots
1 garlic clove, minced
1/2 small bay leaf

1 teaspoon finely chopped thyme or
  1/4 to 1/2 teaspoon dried
  leaf thyme, crumbled
1/8 teaspoon pepper
1-1/2 cups dry white wine

Scrub mussels with a brush to remove sand from shells; rinse well. Remove beards. Discard any mussels that remain open. In a large kettle, melt butter or margarine over medium heat. Add shallots and garlic; sauté until shallots are soft. Add bay leaf, thyme, pepper and wine. Bring to a boil. Reduce heat until liquid barely simmers; add cleaned mussels. Cover kettle; simmer 4 to 8 minutes or until mussels open. Stir with a large spoon after 2 to 3 minutes. Use a slotted spoon to remove cooked mussels. Discard any mussels that do not open. If broth is sandy, strain through several layers of cheesecloth. Serve cooked mussels and broth in individual shallow bowls. Makes 3 to 4 servings.

Poached Salmon with Mushroom Cream

The simple poaching liquid forms a base for a creamy mushroom sauce.

1-1/2 lbs. or 4 (6-oz.) skinless
  salmon fillets
1-1/4 cups finely chopped fresh mushrooms
3 tablespoons finely chopped onion
1-1/4 cups dry white wine
1-1/4 cups water

2/3 cup whipping cream
2 tablespoons butter or margarine
About 3/4 teaspoon finely chopped tarragon
  or 1/4 teaspoon dried leaf tarragon
Salt and pepper

Rinse fish; pat dry with paper towels. If necessary, cut fillets into 4 equal portions. Arrange mushrooms and onion over bottom of a 2-inch-deep stovetop casserole or skillet large enough to hold salmon in a single layer. Arrange salmon over mushrooms and onion. Pour wine and water over salmon. Bring to a boil. Reduce heat; cover and gently simmer about 5 minutes. Undercook salmon slightly; it will continue to cook as it is held. Transfer salmon to a plate. Cover with foil to keep warm. Boil mixture in casserole until liquid is reduced to about 2 cups. Add any juices from salmon on plate. Stir in cream, butter or margarine and tarragon to taste. Boil until reduced to about 1 cup. Season with salt and pepper to taste. Spoon sauce over salmon. Makes 4 servings.

Marinière is French, meaning mariner's style. Mussels and other shellfish are cooked in butter, shallots and white wine. Other seasonings may be added.

Oyster Bundles

Spinach-wrapped oysters served on the half-shell make a beautiful presentation.

2 qts. water	**Ground nutmeg**
30 to 48 large spinach leaves,	**1/2 cup butter or margarine**
stems trimmed	**About 2 teaspoons lemon juice**
24 large oysters	**Finely chopped pimiento or**
Water or bottled clam juice	**red or golden caviar**
Salt and pepper	**1 small lemon, cut in thin wedges**

Pour 2 quarts water into a large saucepan; bring to a boil. Add spinach leaves; cook 30 seconds. Using a slotted spoon, quickly and carefully immerse blanched leaves in ice water. Drain; pat dry with paper towels. Shuck oysters, reserving oyster liquor and bottom shells. Or, ask fish retailer to shuck oysters for you. Scrub reserved shells with a brush; set aside. Strain liquor; combine with enough water or bottled clam juice to make 1-1/2 cups liquid. Pour into a medium saucepan; bring to a simmer. Add shucked oysters; poach 30 to 60 seconds or until oyster edges start to curl and become slightly firm. Drain on paper towels. Lay 1 or 2 blanched spinach leaves on a flat surface. Place a poached oyster about 1 inch from stem-end of leaves. Season lightly with salt, pepper and nutmeg. Fold stem ends over oyster, then fold in both sides. Roll toward tips of leaves, making a neat bundle. If spinach leaves tear, patch with another leaf. Repeat with remaining poached oysters and blanched spinach leaves. Place oyster bundles on reserved shells. Place oyster shells on baking sheets. Refrigerate 3 to 6 hours or proceed with preparation. *Do not refrigerate overnight.* Preheat oven to 350F (175C). Melt butter or margarine in a small saucepan. Stir in lemon juice; keep warm. Bake oyster bundles 3 to 5 minutes or until warmed through. Spoon a little butter-lemon sauce over each. Dot tops with pimiento or caviar. Garnish with lemon wedges. Makes 6 appetizer or 4 main-dish servings.

Amaretto Prawns

Orzo is a rice-shape pasta available in many supermarkets.

16 large or jumbo shrimp	**3/4 cup whipping cream**
(12 to 25 per lb.)	**3 tablespoons brandy**
2 tablespoons butter or margarine	**2 to 3 teaspoons amaretto liqueur**
3/4 teaspoon finely grated lemon peel	**Salt**
3/4 teaspoon finely grated orange peel	**White pepper**
1 tablespoon fresh lemon juice	**Cooked rice or orzo**
2 tablespoon fresh orange juice	

Shell shrimp, leaving tails intact; remove veins. Melt butter or margarine in a large skillet. Add shelled, deveined shrimp, lemon and orange peel, lemon and orange juice, cream, brandy and liqueur. Bring to a boil. Reduce heat; simmer 4 to 5 minutes or until shrimp become firm and turn pink. Sauce will reduce and thicken slightly. If sauce is too thin, remove shrimp and boil sauce until it reduces and thickens. Season with salt and white pepper to taste. Serve with cooked rice or orzo. Makes 4 servings.

How to Make Oyster Bundles

1/Poach shucked oysters until edges start to curl and become slightly firm. Drain on paper towels.

2/Fold stem ends of leaves over oyster. Fold in sides, then roll toward tips of leaves, making a neat bundle.

Beer-Boiled Shrimp   Photo on page 125.

Great finger-food for picnics, outdoor parties or casual suppers.

2 (12-oz.) cans dark beer
1 bay leaf
1-1/2 tablespoons mustard seeds
1/2 teaspoon sugar
1/4 to 1/2 teaspoon dill seeds
1/4 to 1/2 teaspoon dried
   hot red-chili flakes

1/4 teaspoon salt
4 black peppercorns
1-1/2 lbs. medium shrimp, unpeeled
1/4 cup cider vinegar or
   white vinegar
2 garlic cloves, slivered

In a medium saucepan, combine beer, bay leaf, mustard seeds, sugar, dill seeds, chili flakes, salt and peppercorns. Bring to a boil. Reduce heat; simmer 5 minutes. Add shrimp; simmer 2 to 4 minutes or until shrimp become firm and turn pink. Pour cooked shrimp and cooking liquid into a ceramic or glass bowl. Add vinegar and garlic; liquid will become cloudy. Cool to room temperature. Remove and discard bay leaf. Refrigerate until ready to serve; drain. Makes 6 to 8 servings.

Spicy Boiled Crayfish

You'll enjoy this Cajun-style crayfish feast.

4 lbs. live crayfish
Spicy Boil, see below, or
   1 (3-oz.) pkg. crab or shrimp boil
Water
6 to 8 tablespoons fresh lemon juice
2 tablespoons salt

1 large onion, sliced
2 celery stalks, chopped
4 garlic cloves, crushed
6 to 8 parsley sprigs
Butter or margarine, melted

Spicy Boil:
8 whole cloves
6 whole allspice
1 teaspoon dry mustard
5 thyme sprigs or
   1 teaspoon dried leaf thyme

1 teaspoon celery seeds
4 bay leaves, broken in half
6 black peppercorns
About 1-1/2 teaspoon red
   (cayenne) pepper

Rinse crayfish to remove any sand or mud. Place in a large bowl or kettle of cold salted water. Refrigerate up to 1 hour or until ready to cook crayfish. Prepare Spicy Boil, if used. In a 6- to 8-quart kettle, combine Spicy Boil or crab or shrimp boil, 4 quarts water, lemon juice, salt, onion, celery, garlic and parsley. Cover and bring to a boil. Boil gently 15 minutes to let flavors blend. Drop 24 crayfish into boiling liquid. When liquid returns to a boil, cook 4 to 8 minutes, depending on size of crayfish. Like lobster, crayfish will turn bright red when cooked. The best way to test for doneness is to taste the seafood, following directions below on how to eat crayfish. Use a slotted spoon to remove cooked crayfish from boiling liquid. Arrange on a platter. Cook remaining crayfish, adding boiling water, if necessary, to maintain volume of liquid. As soon as cooked crayfish are cool enough to handle, serve with small bowls of melted butter or margarine for dipping. Makes about 4 servings.

Spicy Boil:
Combine all ingredients in a small bowl, adding red pepper to taste. Makes about 3 ounces.

Note: Spicy Boil can also be used when cooking live crab or shrimp.

How to Eat Whole Crayfish

Eating crayfish involves a sense of spirit and both hands. Crayfish connoisseurs spread newspaper on the table and eat straight off the newspaper, not bothering with plates. Provide bibs and a large bowl for shells. Break the tail away from the body with a twisting motion. Most meat is found in the tail. The claws take time and effort to crack, but they contain especially sweet meat. You can also eat the fat or butter and juices from the body cavity.

Spicy Boiled Crayfish

Maryland Blue-Crab Feast

Serve crab heaped on a table covered with newspaper.

1/4 cup seafood seasoning
2 tablespoons salt
2 cups white vinegar

2 cups beer or water
24 live blue crab or other crab
Beer or gingerale

In a large bowl, combine seafood seasoning, salt, vinegar and 2 cups beer or water; blend well. Place 12 crab in a large steamer or pot with a raised rack and tight-fitting lid. Pour one-half of the seasoning liquid over crab. Add remaining crab. Pour remaining liquid over them. Cover and bring liquid to a boil. Steam about 20 minutes. Crab will turn bright red. To serve, spread a table with a thick layer of newspaper. Provide wooden mallets, a paring knife and paper towels. Heap steamed crab in center of table. Serve with beer or gingerale. Makes 4 or 5 servings.

Variation

Other types of crab may be cooked by this method.

Boiled Lobster

A great summertime treat.

Water
4 (about 1-lb.) live Maine lobster or
   other large lobster

Butter or margarine, melted
Lemon wedges
Mayonnaise, page 144, or other mayonnaise

Pour water 6 to 8 inches deep into a large kettle. Cover kettle; bring water to a boil. Grasp a lobster firmly behind the head; plunge head-first into boiling water. Partially cover kettle; bring water back to a simmer. Begin timing when water begins to simmer. Cook 1-pound lobsters 6 to 8 minutes. Add 2 to 3 minutes for each additional pound. Use tongs to remove cooked lobster from kettle; drain on paper towels. Repeat with remaining lobster. Serve cooked lobster warm with butter or margarine and lemon wedges. Or, chill cooked lobster in their shells. Serve with mayonnaise. Provide guests with small forks and pincers to crack shells. Makes 4 servings.

Variation

To steam lobster: Pour about 2 inches sea water or well-salted water into bottom of lobster-pot or a steam-kettle with a perforated top section. Bring water to a boil. Place a live lobster in top section. Cover and steam 8 to 10 minutes for a 1- to 1-1/4-pound lobster, 15 to 18 minutes for a 1-1/2- to 2-pound lobster and 20 to 25 minutes for a 2-1/2- to 5-pound lobster. Use tongs to remove lobster; drain on paper towels. Repeat with remaining lobster.

Cracked Dungeness Crab on Ice

Great party fare featured with one or more sauces.

8 to 12 lbs. in-shell Dungeness crab
   (1 to 1-1/2 lbs. in-shell
   crab per person)
Sauce Rémoulade, page 143

Seafood Cocktail Sauce, page 153
Skordalia, page 149
Cracked ice

Purchase cooked crab or cook live crab as follows. Bring a large kettle of lightly salted water to a boil. Grasp live crab from rear, firmly holding back legs. Drop crab, head first, into boiling water. Reduce heat. Cover and simmer 12 to 20 minutes. Time depends on size of crab. Crab will turn red when done. Drain; set aside until cool enough to handle. Clean and crack crab. Place cracked crab on a large platter. Cover; refrigerate at least 2 hours. Prepare 1 or more sauces. Place cracked ice in a large deep tray or serving bowl. Arrange chilled cracked crab on ice. Provide lobster pincers or nutcrackers and small forks or picks to help pick crab from shells. Serve with sauce. Makes 8 to 10 servings.

Cape Cod Clams

If you dig the clams yourself, they must be purged to get rid of excess sand.

6 dozen steamer clams
1 large onion, chopped
3 garlic cloves, minced
1 cup water
1 cup dry white wine

4 lemon slices
4 parsley sprigs
1 teaspoon salt
1/8 teaspoon pepper
Butter or margarine, melted

Scrub clams with a brush to remove sand from shells. Discard any clams that remain open. Rinse well; place in a large heavy kettle. Add onion, garlic, water, wine, lemon slices, parsley, salt and pepper. Cover tightly; bring to a boil over medium-high heat. Reduce heat until liquid barely simmers. Cook 3 to 5 minutes until clams open. Discard any that do not open. Use a slotted spoon to place clams in a large bowl or serve in individual bowls. Strain cooking liquid through several layers of cheesecloth. Discard onion, garlic, parsley and lemon slices. Serve strained cooking liquid in a serving bowl or individual bowls. To eat, dip each clam in cooking liquid. This washes off any sand and seasons clam. Then dip in melted butter or margarine. Makes 4 to 6 servings.

The most succulent clams for steaming are soft-shell or steamer clams. However, hard-shell clams such as littlenecks, cherrystones, butter and razor clams may be steamed in the same manner. If you dig the clams yourself, they must be purged, page 23, to get rid of excess sand.

Baking & Microwaving

Baking is a simple, quick way to cook fish. It is ideal for stuffed whole fish, such as Fish with Lemon-Rice Stuffing and Salmon-Stuffed Sole. Most recipes call for baking fish in a very hot oven—400F to 450F (205C to 230C). This shortens cooking time and seals in natural juices and flavor.

Fish has little internal fat to keep it moist during cooking. Therefore, it must be protected from dry oven heat. Parmesan Fillets are coated with crumbs and butter. Creole Cod and Sicilian Steaks are covered with a sauce. The baking dish may also be covered to hold in moisture.

Fish can be coated with oil or melted butter to seal in moisture. Sometimes called *oven-frying,* this method doesn't require turning or basting. Easy Garlic-Baked Fillets are coated with a garlic-flavored oil. You'll not only like the flavor, but you'll love the easy preparation.

Enclosing fish and seasonings in parchment paper or foil seals in flavor and moisture, and also protects against dry heat. This simple French technique is called *en papillote,* literally translated *in bag.* Fillets en Papillote are sealed in paper or foil with sensational results. Whole fish, fillets and steaks are equally delicious cooked this easy way.

Microwave cooking is an excellent way to preserve delicate flavor and texture of fish and shellfish. Cooking time is minimal and fish stays moist. There are only three recipes in this chapter that are not adapted for microwave cooking. Instructions are included with all other recipes. For even cooking, be sure to place thick edges or large pieces of fish toward the outside of the cooking dish. Turn the dish a quarter turn once or twice during baking.

Citrus-Sauced Catch

Fish stays moist and tender when cooked in a microwave oven.

1-1/4 to 1-1/2 lbs. any type skinless,
  lean or moderate-fat fish fillets
3 tablespoons butter or margarine, melted
2 tablespoons freshly squeezed orange juice
2 tablespoons lemon juice

1-1/2 tablespoons soy sauce
1 teaspoon finely shredded orange peel
1 teaspoon finely shredded lemon peel
1 small garlic clove, if desired, minced

Purchase 4 individual fillets or cut large fillets into 4 equal portions. Preheat oven to 375F (190C). Butter a baking pan large enough to hold fish in a single layer. Rinse fish; pat dry with paper towels. Arrange fillets in buttered pan. In a small bowl, combine butter or margine and remaining ingredients; drizzle over fish. Cover with foil. Bake 6 to 8 minutes or until fish tests done. Place cooked fish on a platter; drizzle sauce from baking pan over top. Makes 4 servings.

Variation

To microwave: Butter a large glass baking dish. Prepare fish as directed above. Place fish in buttered dish with thickest portions to outside of dish. Combine remaining ingredients; drizzle over fish. Cover with plastic wrap; cut small slits in plastic wrap for steam vents. Microwave on full power (HIGH) 5 to 8 minutes or until fish tests done. Turn dish once during baking. Let stand, covered, 5 minutes before serving. Serve as above.

Whole Catch Sealed-in-Silver

Baking in foil is an easy and tidy way to cook a whole fish.

1 (2-1/2 to 6 lb.) fish, any type,
  scaled, cleaned
Salt and pepper
3 to 4 tablespoons butter or margarine
2 tablespoons finely chopped parsley
1 tablespoon lemon juice

1 tablespoon finely chopped dill,
  or 1 teaspoon dill weed
1 garlic clove, minced
1 or 2 lemons, thinly sliced
1/2 to 1 onion, thinly sliced,
  separated into rings

Ingredients given are for a 2-1/2- to 3-pound fish. Adjust amount of ingredients for larger fish. Preheat oven to 400F (205C). Rinse fish inside and out; pat dry with paper towels. Season inside and out with salt and pepper. Melt butter or margarine in a small saucepan. Stir in parsley, lemon juice, dill and garlic. On a baking sheet, lay a piece of heavy foil large enough to completely enclose fish. Spoon about 1 tablespoon parsley mixture onto foil. Lay seasoned fish on foil. Fill cavity with most of lemon slices and all of onion rings. Spoon about 1 tablespoon parsley mixture over lemon slices and onions. Arrange remaining lemon slices over top of fish. Drizzle with remaining parsley mixture. Bring foil over top of fish. Roll or fold edges, sealing tightly. Bake 7 to 10 minutes per inch of thickness measured at thickest part or until fish tests done. To serve, cut foil open; serve fish and juices directly from foil. Makes 6 to 12 servings.

Note: This recipe is not suitable for cooking in a microwave oven.

Fillets en Papillote

Delicate white fillets sealed in parchment paper or foil and cooked to perfection.

Orange Beurre Blanc, page 146
6 (5- to 6-oz.) skinless pompano,
    turbot, flounder or other lean
    white fish fillets
Salt

White pepper
Finely slivered peel of 1 orange
Finely slivered peel of 1 lemon
2 to 3 tablespoons finely chopped chives or
    green onion tops

Preheat oven to 425F (220C). Prepare Orange Beurre Blanc; set aside. Cut 6 pieces of parchment paper or foil into heart shapes measuring about 12 inches long and 10 inches at widest point. Paper or foil must be at least 3 inches longer than fish. Butter paper or foil. Place 1 fillet on right half of each heart. Season with salt and white pepper. Sprinkle on orange peel, lemon peel and chopped chives or green onion tops. Fold left half of each heart over fish, matching edges. Starting at top of heart, seal cases by folding edge in 2 or 3 narrow folds. Twist tip of heart to hold case closed. Place on a large ungreased baking sheet. Bake 6 to 8 minutes. Gently reheat Orange Beurre Blanc; pour into a small bowl or sauceboat. To serve fish, place 1 packet on each of 6 serving plates. Cut cases open by slashing a large **X** on top of each; fold back paper or foil. Serve with Orange Beurre Blanc. Makes 6 servings.

Variation

To microwave: Prepare fish in parchment paper, not foil, as directed above. Place in microwave with thickest portions to outside. Microwave on full power (HIGH) 5 to 8 minutes or until fish tests done. Turn once during baking. Serve as above.

Hickory-Smoked Fish

Liquid smoke gives this delicious fish its delicate hickory flavor.

2 cups water
1 cup natural-hickory liquid smoke
6 (4- to 8-oz.) firm, skinless
    fish fillets, steaks or chunks

Salt and pepper
1/4 cup butter or margarine
Lemon wedges, if desired

Preheat oven to 375F (190C). Arrange fish in a shallow dish large enough to hold fish in a single layer. Combine water and liquid smoke; pour over fish. Marinate 15 minutes. If liquid does not cover fish, turn once. Drain off marinade. Lightly season marinated fish with salt and pepper. Lightly butter a baking dish large enough to hold fish in a single layer. Arrange fish in buttered dish. Cut butter or margarine into small pieces; sprinkle over fish. Cover with foil. Bake 6 to 8 minutes per inch of thickness measured at thickest part or until fish tests done. Or, insert a rapid-response thermometer at thickest part of fish; temperature should reach 140F (60C). Serve with lemon wedges, if desired. Makes 6 servings.

Variation

To microwave: Butter a large glass baking dish. Place marinated fish in buttered dish with thickest portions to outside of dish. Dot with butter or margarine. Cover with plastic wrap; cut small slits in plastic wrap for steam vents. Microwave on full power (HIGH) 6 to 8 minutes or until fish tests done. Turn dish once during baking. Serve as above.

How to Make Fillets en Papillote

1/Lay fish on one side of parchment or foil hearts; fold paper or foil over fish. Fold sides of paper or foil together to seal; twist ends.

2/Cut cases open by slashing a large X on top of each; fold back paper or foil. Serve with Orange Beurre Blanc, page 146.

Shark with Lime-Cumin Marinade

Excellent for low-sodium, low-calorie dieters.

4 (6- to 8-oz.) shark, swordfish, haddock, sea bass, halibut or other lean fish steaks
Finely shredded peel of 1 lime

1/4 cup fresh lime juice
1/2 teaspoon ground cumin
1-1/2 tablespoons vegetable oil
10 to 12 cilantro sprigs, if desired

Rinse steaks; pat dry with paper towels. In a plastic food-storage bag, combine lime peel, lime juice, cumin and oil. If desired, chop 5 or 6 cilantro sprigs; add to juice mixture. Reserve remaining cilantro for garnish. Place fish in bag; close bag. Refrigerate about 1 hour. Preheat oven to 450F (230C). Grease a baking dish large enough to hold fish in a single layer. Arrange fish in greased dish. Pour marinade over top; cover with foil. Bake 8 to 10 minutes or until fish tests done. Arrange baked fish on a platter; garnish with reserved cilantro, if desired. Makes 4 servings.

Variation

To microwave: Grease a large glass baking dish. Arrange fish with thickest portions to outside of greased dish. Pour marinade over top. Cover with plastic wrap; cut small slits in plastic wrap for steam vents. Microwave on full power (HIGH) 5 to 8 minutes or until fish tests done. Turn dish twice during baking. Serve as above.

Seafood Pinwheels with Havarti Sauce

Simple to prepare and simply elegant to present.

1-1/2 lbs. skinless sand dab, sole,
   pompano or other lean white
   fish fillets
Salt
White pepper
Juice of 1/2 lemon
1 egg yolk

About 1/3 cup milk
4 oz. Danish Havarti cheese,
   shredded
1 to 2 teaspoons finely chopped dill or
   1/4 to 1/2 teaspoon dill weed
4 watercress or dill sprigs

Preheat oven to 450F (230C). Gently rinse fillets; pat dry with paper towels. Season with salt and white pepper; sprinkle with lemon juice. Cut seasoned fillets into 20 strips, 5 to 6 inches long and 1 to 1-1/2 inches wide. Roll up each strip like a pinwheel; secure with wooden picks. Oil a 13" x 9" baking dish. Arrange fish pinwheels in a single layer in oiled dish; set aside. In top of a double boiler, beat egg yolk and 1/3 cup milk until blended. Place over simmering water and cook, stirring constantly, until mixture thickens enough to coat a spoon. Add cheese and dill; continue to cook and stir until cheese is melted. Cover surface of sauce with waxed paper; set aside. Bake fish pinwheels 5 to 8 minutes or until fish tests done; drain on paper towels. Reserve fish juices in dish. Carefully remove wooden picks from cooked fish. Arrange 5 pinwheels on each of 4 warm plates. Reheat cheese sauce, if necessary; stir in 2 to 4 tablespoons liquid from baking dish. Thin sauce with more liquid or milk, if necessary. Spoon sauce over and around pinwheels. Garnish with watercress or dill sprigs. Makes 4 servings.

Variation

To microwave: Butter a large glass baking dish. Arrange fish pinwheels around outside of buttered dish. Cover with plastic wrap; cut small slits in plastic wrap for steam vents. Microwave on full power (HIGH) 4 to 8 minutes or until fish tests done. Turn dish once during baking. Serve as above.

Parmesan Fillets

This savory dish is quick and easy to prepare.

1 (1-lb.) pkg. frozen pollock, cod,
   haddock, ocean perch or
   halibut fillets
1-1/2 tablespoons fine dry breadcrumbs
1/4 cup freshly grated Parmesan cheese

Pinch of salt
1/3 cup milk
2 tablespoons butter or margarine, melted
3 or 4 lemon wedges

Let fish stand at room temperature 20 minutes; do not thaw completely. Preheat oven to 450F (230C). Butter a baking dish large enough to hold fish in a single layer; set aside. Cut fish into 3 or 4 equal portions. On a plate, combine breadcrumbs, cheese and salt. Pour milk into a shallow dish. Dip fish portions in milk, then roll in crumb mixture to coat. Arrange coated fish in buttered dish; drizzle with butter or margarine. Bake 20 to 25 minutes or until fish tests done. Serve with lemon wedges. Makes 3 to 4 servings.

Note: This recipe is not suitable for cooking in a microwave oven.

Seafood Pinwheels with Havarti Sauce

How to Make Salmon-Stuffed Sole

1/With a knife, cut off head on a diagonal from behind gills to behind vent. Remove viscera. Rinse fish.

2/With white belly-side up, use a filleting knife to cut fillet away from backbone and ribs.

3/Bend middle section of fish until backbone snaps in 2 or 3 places. Remove sections of backbone and ribs.

4/Salt and pepper inside of fish; fill with salmon mixture. Bake 15 minutes or until fish tests done.

Salmon-Stuffed Sole

Slivers of fresh basil in the sauce give color and flavor.

1/2 lb. skinless salmon fillets,
   cut into 1-inch pieces
1 egg white
3/4 cup whipping cream
Salt and white pepper

1 (2-1/2- to 3-lb.) or
   2 (1-1/2- to 2-lb.) sole or
   other flatfish
Tomato-Basil Beurre Blanc, see below
Parsley or watercress sprigs

Tomato-Basil Beurre Blanc:
1 shallot, minced
2-1/2 tablespoons white-wine vinegar
1/4 cup dry white wine
1/2 cup butter or margarine,
   room temperature

1 medium tomato, peeled,
   seeded, finely chopped
2 tablespoons finely sliced basil leaves
Salt
White pepper

Preheat oven to 350F (175C). In a blender or food processor fitted with a metal blade, process salmon pieces to a fine paste. Add egg white; process until blended. With motor running, slowly add cream until absorbed. Add salt and white pepper to taste. Trim tail of fish. Scale fish. Lay fish, dark-side up, on a flat surface. Remove dark skin if desired, or remove skin after fish is baked. Using kitchen shears, trim fins but do not cut off completely. With a knife, cut off head on a diagonal from behind gills to behind vent. Remove viscera. Rinse fish. Lay fish white-side down; pull out any roe. Using a small sharp knife, cut through flesh, midway between anal and dorsal fins, from head to tail. Carefully insert knife between flesh and bones; partially cut upper fillet away from backbone and ribs. Fold fillets back, away from ribs. To remove backbone and ribs, bend middle section of fish until backbone snaps in 2 or 3 places. Remove sections of backbone with ribs attached. Leave anal- and dorsal-fin bones on each side to support fish. Salt and pepper pocket inside of fish; fill with salmon mixture. Fold fillets over salmon mixture. Butter a baking dish large enough to hold fish. Place stuffed fish in buttered dish. Butter foil or parchment paper large enough to cover fish; place over fish but not around dish. Bake 15 minutes or until fish tests done. While fish bakes, prepare Tomato-Basil Beurre Blanc. Carefully lift baked fish from baking dish to a platter. Pull off fin bones on either side of fish. Garnish with parsley or watercress. Spoon some of sauce over baked fish. Pour remaining sauce into a bowl; serve separately. To serve fish, slice crosswise. Makes 6 servings.

Tomato-Basil Beurre Blanc:
In a medium saucepan, combine shallot, vinegar and wine. Boil gently until reduced to 2 tablespoons. Reduce heat to low. Whisk in butter or margarine, a little at a time, until sauce becomes thick and creamy. Whisk constantly, removing from heat occasionally to prevent separation. Stir in tomato and basil. Season with salt and white pepper. Makes 1-1/2 cups.

Variation

To microwave: Prepare salmon stuffing and fish as directed. Place stuffed fish in a buttered glass baking dish. Brush fish with melted butter. Cover loosely with buttered waxed paper. Microwave on full power (HIGH) 8 to 14 minutes or until fish tests done. Turn dish once during baking. Serve as above.

Baked Salt Cod with Potatoes & Fennel

Dried salt cod is often sold in wooden boxes. It must be soaked before cooking.

1 lb. salt cod
Water
1/4 cup white-wine vinegar
9 tablespoons olive oil
2 medium onions, thinly sliced,
   separated into rings
2 garlic cloves, minced
1-1/2 teaspoons finely chopped rosemary or
   1/2 to 3/4 teaspoon dried
   leaf rosemary

1/4 teaspoon finely chopped thyme or
   1/4 teaspoon dried leaf thyme
3 medium, new potatoes, cooked, peeled,
   thinly sliced
Salt
Freshly ground pepper
1/4 cup chopped parsley
1 teaspoon fennel seeds, crushed
1/2 cup fresh breadcrumbs
Herb-Tomato Sauce, see below

Herb-Tomato Sauce:
2 (14-1/2-oz.) cans Italian-style tomatoes
1/4 cup olive oil
1 small onion, chopped
1/4 cup dry white wine or vermouth
3/4 teaspoon finely chopped thyme or
   1/4 teaspoon dried leaf thyme

3/4 teaspoon finely chopped rosemary or
   1/4 teaspoon dried leaf rosemary
1/4 teaspoon sugar
Salt and pepper

Place salt cod in a large bowl. Cover with cold water; refrigerate 24 hours, changing water several times. Drain. Break cod into chunks; place in a large saucepan. Cover with cold water; bring to a boil. Reduce heat; simmer 7 to 10 minutes or until cod tests done. Drain. Remove bones; coarsely flake cooked cod. In a bowl, toss flaked cod with vinegar; set aside. Preheat oven to 375F (190C). Heat 2 tablespoons olive oil in a large skillet. Add onion rings; sauté until golden, 8 to 10 minutes. Stir in garlic, rosemary and thyme. Lightly grease a 9-inch-square baking dish. Spread one-third of onion mixture in greased dish. Top with half of flaked cod. Arrange half of potatoes on top. Season with salt and pepper. Drizzle with 3 tablespoons olive oil. Sprinkle with parsley and fennel seeds. Repeat layers. Top with remaining onion mixture. Combine breadcrumbs and remaining 1 tablespoon olive oil. Sprinkle over top of layered ingredients. Bake, uncovered, until casserole is hot and top is browned, about 25 minutes. Meanwhile, prepare Herb-Tomato Sauce. Pour into a bowl; serve separately. Makes 6 servings.

Herb-Tomato Sauce:
In a blender or food processor fitted with a metal blade, process tomatoes with juice until smooth. Heat olive oil in a large skillet. Add onion; sauté until limp. Add wine or vermouth; cook until liquid evaporates. Add pureed tomatoes, thyme, rosemary and sugar. Add salt and pepper to taste. Cook 5 minutes over high heat, stirring occasionally. Reduce heat to medium; cook 5 to 10 minutes longer or until medium thick. Makes 2 cups.

Note: This recipe is not suitable for cooking in a microwave oven.

When buying salt cod, look for thick, smooth, supple pieces. The salt shouldn't flake off when pressed. Salt cod with the bone in must be soaked a little longer than boneless salt cod. Remove the bones and skin before using.

Salmon Scallops with Sorrel Sauce

Sorrel *is a leafy green that has a tart-lemony flavor. It is easy to grow at home.*

3 (8-oz.) skinless salmon fillets,
   about 1 inch thick
2 tablespoons butter or margarine, melted
Salt
White pepper
2 cups Fish Stock, page 101, or
   2 (8-oz.) bottles clam juice

1/2 cup dry white wine
4 oz. sorrel
1 cup whipping cream
2 tablespoons butter or margarine,
   room temperature
2 tablespoons salmon caviar, if desired
6 watercress or parsley sprigs

Preheat oven to 425F (220C). Lightly oil 1 or 2 baking sheets large enough to hold fillets in a single layer. Cut salmon fillets in half horizontally, making 6 (1/2-inch-thick) salmon scallops. If scallops are not of even thickness, place each scallop between 2 lightly oiled pieces of waxed paper; gently pound with smooth side of a meat mallet to make even. Brush scallops with 2 tablespoons melted butter or margarine, covering both sides. Season lightly with salt and white pepper. Arrange in a single layer on oiled baking sheets; set aside. In a medium saucepan, bring Fish Stock or clam juice and wine to a boil. Gently boil until reduced to 1/2 cup. Wash sorrel; remove stems and thick central veins. Stack 8 to 10 sorrel leaves; tightly roll together. Cut in thin crosswise shreds. Repeat with remaining leaves, making about 3 cups loosely packed, finely shredded sorrel. Stir cream into reduced fish stock; simmer several minutes until slightly thickened. Add sorrel; cook about 30 seconds. Remove from heat; stir in 2 tablespoons butter or margarine. Season with salt and white pepper to taste. Meanwhile, bake salmon scallops 2 to 4 minutes or until fish tests done. To serve, pour about 1/4 cup sauce into each of 6 shallow serving bowls. Place cooked scallops on sauce. Garnish each with 1 teaspoon caviar, if desired, and watercress or parsley. Makes 6 servings.

Variation

To microwave: Butter a large glass baking dish. Prepare fish as directed above. Place salmon scallops in buttered dish. Cover with plastic wrap; cut small slits in plastic wrap for steam vents. Microwave on full power (HIGH) 2 to 3 minutes or until fish tests done. Turn dish once during baking. Serve as above.

How Much to Buy

For whole fish, allow 3/4 to 1 pound per serving. For fillets and steaks, allow 4 to 8 ounces per serving. Half the total weight of a roundfish is bone, head and tail. About 1/3 the total weight of flatfish is edible.

Refrigerate salt cod while it is soaking. Once it takes on water, it must be treated as fresh fish. It will spoil rapidly.

Sicilian Steaks

The robust sauce complements these firm, meat-like steaks.

**6 swordfish, shark, tuna, wahoo or
   mahi mahi steaks**

**Salt and pepper
Sicilian Sauce, see below**

Sicilian Sauce:

2 tablespoons olive oil
**1 medium onion, thinly sliced,
   separated into rings**
**4 small tomatoes, peeled, seeded, chopped,
   or 1 (16-oz.) can whole peeled
   tomatoes, drained, chopped**
1/4 cup sliced pimiento-stuffed olives

1/4 cup pine nuts, lightly toasted
1/4 cup raisins
2 teaspoons capers
2 garlic cloves, minced
4 or 5 drops hot-pepper sauce, or to taste
Salt and pepper

Preheat oven to 450F (230C). Rinse fish; pat dry with paper towels. Season lightly with salt and pepper. Oil a baking dish large enough to hold fish in a single layer. Arrange fish in oiled dish. Prepare Sicilian Sauce; spoon over fish. Cover with foil. Bake 10 to 12 minutes or until fish tests done. Makes 6 servings.

Sicilian Sauce:

Heat oil in a skillet. Add onion rings; sauté 2 to 3 minutes. Add fresh or canned tomatoes, olives, pine nuts, raisins, capers, garlic and hot-pepper sauce. Cook 5 minutes over medium-low heat, stirring occasionally. Season with salt and pepper to taste. Makes about 3 cups.

Variation

To microwave: Oil a large glass baking dish. Prepare fish as directed above. Arrange fish with thickest portions to outside of oiled dish. Spoon sauce over top. Cover with plastic wrap; cut small slits in plastic wrap for steam vents. Microwave on full power (HIGH) 5 to 10 minutes or until fish tests done. Turn dish twice during baking.

The quality of frozen fish can be very good. Use frozen, if possible; partially thaw, if necessary. One of the keys to handling frozen fish is to thaw it in the coldest part of your refrigerator. Do not thaw it completely or it may become dry when cooked. See page 7.

Creole Cod

Serve this Louisiana specialty with hot buttered rice.

2 (1-lb.) pkgs. frozen cod fillets or
  2 lbs. fresh cod fillets
Salt and black pepper
2 medium tomatoes, peeled, seeded, chopped,
  or 1 (16-oz.) can whole peeled
  tomatoes, drained, chopped

1 medium, green bell pepper, diced
1 small onion, chopped
3/4 cup sliced ripe olives
6 tablespoons butter or margarine
3 tablespoons lemon juice
1/4 teaspoon hot-pepper sauce, or to taste

To use frozen cod, let stand at room temperature 20 minutes; do not thaw completely. Preheat oven to 450F (230C). Cut each partially frozen fish block into 3 portions. *To use fresh cod,* cut into 6 equal portions. Butter a baking dish large enough to hold fish in a single layer. Arrange partially thawed or fresh fish in buttered dish. Season with salt and black pepper. Spread fresh or canned tomatoes, green pepper, onion and olives over fish. In a small saucepan, melt butter or margarine. Stir in lemon juice and hot-pepper sauce; drizzle over fish. Cover with foil. Bake partially thawed fish 20 to 25 minutes and fresh fish 7 to 10 minutes or until fish tests done. Makes 6 servings.

Variation

To microwave: Arrange fish pieces in a buttered glass baking dish. Prepare as above. Cover with plastic wrap; cut small slits in plastic wrap for steam vents. *Microwave partially thawed fish* on full power (HIGH) 11 to 14 minutes or until fish tests done. Turn dish twice during baking. *Microwave fresh or fully thawed fish* 5 to 8 minutes or until fish tests done. Turn dish once during backing.

Sole Michelle

Simplicity is sublime with this sophisticated dish.

Lime-Ginger-Butter Sauce, page 148
6 (6-oz.) skinless sole or
  pompano fillets
Salt
White pepper

3 tablespoons butter or
  margarine, melted
1 cup sliced almonds, lightly toasted
Lime slices

Prepare Lime-Ginger-Butter Sauce. Preheat oven to 450F (230C). Rinse fish; pat dry with paper towels. Season with salt and white pepper. Butter a large baking sheet. Brush fish with melted butter or margarine. Place on buttered baking sheet. Press almonds onto top side of fillets, covering completely. Bake 6 to 8 minutes or until fish tests done. Arrange cooked fillets on a platter. Spoon Lime-Ginger-Butter Sauce over fish. Garnish with lime slices. Makes 6 servings.

Variation

To microwave: Butter a large glass baking dish. Prepare fish as directed above. Place fish in buttered dish with thickest portions to outside of dish; top with almonds. Cover with plastic wrap; cut small slits in plastic wrap for steam vents. Microwave on full power (HIGH) 4 to 7 minutes or until fish tests done. Turn dish once during baking. Serve as above.

Salmon with Lemon-Rice Stuffing, page 62

Fish with Lemon-Rice Stuffing   Photo on page 61.

Lemon flavors this delicious stuffing—perfect for a fisherman's prize catch.

Lemon-Rice Stuffing, see below
Large whole fish, any size or type,
   cleaned, scaled

Salt and pepper
Butter or margarine, melted

Lemon-Rice Stuffing for 6 to 8 lb. fish:

1/4 cup butter or margarine
3/4 cup chopped celery
1/2 cup chopped onion
1/4 cup slivered almonds
3 cups cooked rice
1 cup coarsely chopped mushrooms
1/2 cup dairy sour cream

2 teaspoons finely shredded lemon peel
1/4 cup finely chopped peeled lemon
3 tablespoons finely chopped parsley
1 teaspoon paprika
1/4 to 1/2 teaspoon dried leaf thyme
Salt and pepper

Preheat oven to 375F (190C). Prepare Lemon-Rice Stuffing. Grease a shallow baking dish large enough to hold fish; set aside. Rinse fish inside and out; pat dry with paper towels. Cut off head and tail, if desired, or trim tail. Season inside and out with salt and pepper. Stuff fish with Lemon-Rice Stuffing. Close opening with small skewers or wooden picks, lacing with heavy thread or kitchen string, if desired, or sew closed with heavy thread. Place fish in greased dish. Turn tail-end up, if necessary. Brush fish with butter or margarine. Bake, uncovered, 8 to 10 minutes per inch of thickness measured at thickest part or until fish tests done. Or, insert a thermometer at thickest part of fish; temperature should reach 140F (60C). Baste fish occasionally with melted butter or margarine. Carefully lift cooked fish to a platter. Pull out fins. Cut down center back of cooked fish to backbone and ribs. Using a knife, separate upper fillet from backbone. Cut upper fillet into serving pieces. To serve, slide a wide metal spatula between flesh and ribs. Lift off each serving; place on individual plates or a platter. When top fillet has been removed, remove and discard backbone and ribs. Cut and serve remaining fillet, spoon stuffing onto individual plates or into a bowl. Makes about 1 serving per pound of fish.

Lemon-Rice Stuffing:
Melt butter or margarine in a medium skillet. Add celery, onion and almonds; sauté until celery and onions are tender. In a large bowl, combine sautéed onion mixture, rice, mushrooms, sour cream, lemon peel, chopped lemon, parsley, paprika and thyme. Stir in salt and pepper to taste. Makes about 6 cups.

Variations

Increase stuffing quantity for larger fish, decrease quantity for smaller fish, or bake extra stuffing in a covered casserole.

If fish weighs more than 6 pounds, compare size to oven. If fish is too long for oven, cut fish in half crosswise. Bake halves, unstuffed, side by side. Bake stuffing in a covered casserole. After baking, reassemble fish; disguise cut with a row of parsley or watercress. Serve stuffing separately.

To microwave: Whole fish, weighing no more than 2-1/2 to 3 pounds, can be stuffed and baked in the microwave. Stuff fish; close with wooden picks or sew closed. Place stuffed fish in a greased glass dish. Cover with plastic wrap; cut small slits in plastic wrap for steam vents. Microwave on full power (HIGH) 10 to 14 minutes or until fish tests done. Turn dish once during baking. Serve as above.

How to Make Fish with Lemon-Rice Stuffing

1/Season fish inside and out with salt and pepper. Spoon Lemon-Rice Stuffing into body cavity.

2/Close stuffed fish with small skewers or wooden picks, or sew closed with heavy thread.

Slender Fillets

This low-calorie dish cooks quickly.

1-1/2 lbs. skinless lean cod, catfish, pike, lingcod, perch, rockfish or sea bass fillets
Salt and pepper
2 tablespoons thawed orange-juice concentrate

1 tablespoon finely shredded orange peel
1 tablespoon vegetable oil
1/8 teaspoon ground nutmeg

Preheat oven to 375F (190C). Rinse fish; pat dry with paper towels. Cut rinsed fish into 4 to 6 servings. Season with salt and pepper. Lightly oil a baking pan large enough to hold fish in a single layer. Arrange seasoned fish in oiled pan. In a small bowl, combine orange-juice concentrate, orange peel, oil and nutmeg; spoon over seasoned fish. Cover with foil. Bake 6 to 10 minutes or until fish tests done. Makes 4 to 6 servings.

Variation

To microwave: Prepare fish and sauce as directed above. Arrange seasoned fish in an oiled glass baking dish. Spoon sauce over top. Cover with plastic wrap; cut small slits in plastic wrap for steam vents. Microwave on full power (HIGH) 4 to 6 minutes or until fish tests done. Turn dish once during baking.

Creamy Herbed Salmon

A creamy mushroom sauce accents this quick-to-prepare salmon.

2 tablespoons butter or margarine
1 teaspoon finely chopped dill or
   1/4 teaspoon dill weed
2 teaspoons lemon juice
4 (6- to 8-oz.) salmon steaks

Salt
Freshly ground pepper
4 rosemary or parsley sprigs,
   if desired
1/4 cup whipping cream

Preheat oven to 375F (190C). Place butter or margarine and dill in a 9-inch-square baking pan. Place in preheated oven until butter or margarine melts. Stir in lemon juice. Gently rinse salmon; pat dry with paper towels. Season with salt and pepper. Arrange seasoned salmon in a single layer in baking pan, turning to coat both sides. Top each salmon steak with a rosemary or parsley sprig, if desired. Bake 6 to 10 minutes or until fish tests done. Place cooked salmon steaks on a platter; keep warm. Pour juices from pan into a small saucepan. Stir in cream. Stir over medium heat until sauce boils; season with salt and pepper to taste. Spoon sauce over cooked fish. Makes 4 servings.

Variation

To microwave: Place butter or margarine and dill in a 9-inch-square glass baking dish. Microwave on full power (HIGH) about 20 seconds to melt butter or margarine. Stir in lemon juice. Prepare salmon as directed above; arrange in baking dish, turning to coat both sides. Top each steak with a rosemary or parsley sprig, if desired. Cover dish with waxed paper. Microwave on full power (HIGH) about 4 minutes or until fish tests done. Place cooked fish on a platter; keep warm. Stir cream into juices in dish. Microwave on full power (HIGH) about 2 minutes or until sauce boils. Stir sauce to blend; season with salt and pepper to taste. Spoon sauce over cooked fish.

Easy Garlic-Baked Fillets

Guests will never guess this dish is so quick and easy to prepare.

1/4 cup vegetable oil
2 large garlic cloves, crushed
1-1/4 to 1-1/2 lbs. skinless sablefish,
   croaker, flounder or turbot fillets

Salt and black pepper
Paprika
Red (cayenne) pepper
4 lemon or lime wedges, if desired

Preheat oven to 450F (230C). Lightly oil a baking sheet large enough to hold fish in a single layer; set aside. Heat oil in a small saucepan. Add garlic; sauté about 5 minutes. Do not let garlic brown; discard sautéed garlic. Cut fish fillets into 4 equal servings. Generously brush both sides of fillets with garlic-seasoned oil. Season with salt and black pepper. Arrange seasoned fillets in a single layer on oiled baking sheet. Dust tops with paprika and red pepper. Bake 6 to 8 minutes or until fish tests done. Serve with lemon or lime wedges, if desired. Makes 4 servings.

Variation

To microwave: Grease a large glass baking dish. Brush fish with garlic-seasoned oil; arrange with thickest portions to outside of greased dish. Dust with paprika and red pepper. Cover with buttered waxed paper. Microwave on full power (HIGH) 4 to 8 minutes or until fish tests done. Turn dish once during baking. Serve as above.

Crab Imperial

An all-time favorite traditional dish.

1/4 cup butter or margarine
1 small onion, finely chopped
2 tablespoons all-purpose flour
1/8 teaspoon red (cayenne) pepper
1/8 teaspoon ground nutmeg
1/2 cup milk
1/2 cup half and half
About 2 tablespoons dry sherry
1/4 cup Mayonnaise, page 144,
　or other mayonnaise

About 2 teaspoons lemon juice
Salt
1 lb. crabmeat
3 to 4 tablespoons freshly grated
　Parmesan cheese
1/4 to 1/2 teaspoon paprika, if desired
6 to 8 lemon wedges

Preheat oven to 450F (230C). Butter a 1-quart casserole or 6 to 8 small au gratin dishes, scallop shells or empty blue-crab shells; set aside. Melt 2 tablespoons butter or margarine in a medium saucepan. Add onion; sauté about 5 minutes. Blend in flour, red pepper and nutmeg. Cook 1 to 2 minutes, stirring constantly. Stir in milk, half and half and 2 tablespoons sherry. Cook until thick and smooth, 3 to 4 minutes. Stir in mayonnaise, 2 teaspoons lemon juice and salt. Taste and add more sherry, lemon juice and salt, if desired. Set aside. Melt remaining 2 tablespoons butter or margarine in a large skillet. Flake crabmeat; remove cartilage. Add flaked crabmeat to skillet. Stirring occasionally, cook over low heat 1 minute or until heated through. Gently fold in sauce. Spoon mixture into buttered casserole, small dishes or shells. Sprinkle top with Parmesan cheese and paprika, if desired. Bake 12 to 15 minutes or until mixture is lightly browned and bubbling. Serve with lemon wedges. Makes 6 to 8 servings.

Variation

To microwave: Butter microwave-safe dish or dishes listed above. Prepare crabmeat mixture as directed above. Cover with waxed paper. Microwave on full power (HIGH) 5 to 8 minutes until mixture bubbles. Mixture will not brown; sprinkle with paprika for color. Serve as above.

Large scallop shells—real or made from porcelain—are often used for cooking and serving scallops. They can be purchased at kitchenware shops and are attractive for presenting all kinds of shellfish.

Sautéing, Pan-Frying & Deep-Frying

Frying is the most popular way to cook fish and shellfish. Trout, chum or pink salmon, flounder and other low- or moderate-fat, firm-texture fish are best for frying. High-fat fish, such as bluefish and tuna, are too rich to fry. They are best grilled, baked or broiled. Shellfish also fry well.

Sautéing and *pan-frying* use small amounts of oil, clarified butter, or a combination of butter or margarine and oil. Plain butter and margarine smoke at a low temperature, hence the addition of oil. *Deep-frying* means cooking in a deep layer of vegetable oil or melted vegetable shortening. Use a heavy saucepan, wok or deep-fryer.

Sautéed foods are not coated. Pan-fried foods are coated with flour, cornmeal or crumbs. Trout Meunière with Pecans is dipped in milk, then in flour to coat it. Rocky Mountain Trout is coated with a cornmeal mixture. Coatings keep fish moist during frying and give it a delicious crispness. However, seafood breaded too far in advance of cooking will become soggy and sticky. Fish or shrimp can be coated with Beer Batter or another batter before deep-frying. The beer lightens the batter and gives a crisp coating. If fat is at the correct temperature when seafood is added, a crust forms almost immediately, holding in juices and preventing fat from soaking in.

Use a neutral-flavor vegetable oil or shortening that can be heated to at least 375F (190C) without smoking. When deep-frying, use enough oil or shortening to float the fish, but don't fill the fryer more than half-full. Place a small amount of fish at a time into the hot oil, so the pieces don't touch. This prevents the temperature of the fat from dropping suddenly and assures thorough cooking and even browning. Cooking time varies depending on size, volume and temperature of fish and size of fryer.

Almond-Sole Meunière

An uncomplicated, yet lovely way to serve fish fillets.

4 (5- to 6-oz.) sole, flounder or
    other skinless, thin, lean,
    white fish fillets
Salt and pepper
3 tablespoons butter or margarine
1 to 2 tablespoons vegetable oil

1/3 cup sliced almonds
1-1/2 teaspoons finely shredded lemon or
    lime peel
1-1/2 tablespoons lemon or lime juice
2 or 3 parsley sprigs
4 lemon or lime wedges

Preheat oven to 165F (75C). Rinse fillets; pat dry with paper towels. Season with salt and pepper. Heat 1 tablespoon butter or margarine and 1 tablespoon oil in a large skillet. Add seasoned fillets. Over medium heat, cook 2 minutes on each side or until fish tests done, adding more oil, if needed. Arrange cooked fish on a platter; cover with foil. Keep warm in oven. Add remaining 2 tablespoons butter or margarine and almonds to skillet. Sauté 2 to 3 minutes or until almonds are lightly toasted. Stir in lemon or lime peel and lemon or lime juice. Spoon sauce over fillets. Garnish with parsley sprigs and lemon or lime wedges. Serve immediately. Makes 4 servings.

Pan Fish

One of the simplest ways to cook small whole fish.

4 (6- to 12-oz.) butterfish,
    pompano, spot, yellow perch
    or other small whole fish,
    cleaned, scaled
Salt and pepper
1/4 to 1/2 cup all-purpose flour or
    fine, dry breadcrumbs

About 1/4 cup butter or margarine
About 2 tablespoons vegetable oil
1 lemon, cut in half
Chopped parsley or other chopped herbs

Rinse fish; pat dry with paper towels. Remove heads, if desired. Season with salt and pepper. Coat with flour or breadcrumbs. Heat 1/4 cup butter or margarine and 2 tablespoons oil in a large skillet. Add coated fish; pan-fry over medium-high heat 2 to 4 minutes until browned on each side, turning carefully. Add more butter or margarine and oil, if necessary. Squeeze lemon juice over fish. Arrange cooked fish on a platter or serve from skillet. Sprinkle with parsley or other herbs. Makes 4 servings.

Beer Batter

Use to coat fish or shrimp that will be deep-fried.

2 eggs, separated
3/4 cup beer
1 tablespoon vegetable oil

1 cup all-purpose flour
1/2 teaspoon salt

In a medium bowl, beat together egg yolks, beer, oil, flour and salt until smooth. Let stand 3 to 6 hours. When ready to use, in a small bowl, beat egg whites until stiff but not dry. Gently fold beaten egg whites into batter. Makes 2-1/2 cups.

Fish & Chips

Traditionally, this British snack is served in cones of newspaper.

5 medium potatoes, unpeeled (1-1/2 lbs.)
1-1/2 lbs. skinless sea bass, lingcod or
   other firm-texture fillets
Vegetable oil for deep-frying
1 cup all-purpose flour
1/2 teaspoon salt

1/2 teaspoon baking powder
1 egg
1 cup milk
Lemon wedges
Malt or cider vinegar
Salt

Cut potatoes lengthwise in 1/2-inch-thick French-fry strips; set aside. Cut fish in 1-1/2- to 2-inch pieces; set aside. In a wok, deep-fat fryer or heavy saucepan, heat oil to 365F (185C) or until a 1-inch cube of bread turns golden brown in 1 minute. Preheat oven to 165F (75C). Fill a wire frying basket one-fourth full with potato strips. Slowly lower basket into hot oil. If oil bubbles excessively, raise and lower basket several times. Deep-fry potatoes 5 to 7 minutes or until golden. Drain potatoes on paper towels, then arrange on a large baking sheet. Heat oil again to 365F (185C). Fry remaining potatoes in 3 batches. Remove basket; do not use basket for frying fish. Pat fish dry with paper towels. In a medium bowl, combine flour, salt, baking powder, egg and milk. Beat with a fork until smooth. Dip fish into batter; let excess batter drip back into bowl. Fry 4 or 5 coated fish pieces at a time, 3 to 5 minutes or until golden brown. Drain on paper towels. Keep warm in oven until all pieces are cooked. Remove fish from oven. Broil potatoes, 6 inches from heat, 2 to 3 minutes or until crisp. Arrange fried fish and chips on a large platter; garnish with lemon wedges. Serve with vinegar and salt for sprinkling on fish and chips. Makes 4 to 6 servings.

Rosemary-Scented Fish Steaks

The Greek-inspired flavors of rosemary and garlic complement fish steaks.

4 (6-oz.) swordfish, grouper, sea trout,
   sea bass or hake steaks
Salt and pepper
2 to 4 tablespoons all-purpose flour
3 tablespoons olive oil
2 garlic cloves, minced

1 teaspoon chopped rosemary or
   1/4 teaspoon dried leaf rosemary,
   crumbled
2 tablespoons white-wine vinegar
2 tablespoons water
Pinch of sugar

Rinse fish; pat dry with paper towels. Season with salt and pepper; dust lightly with flour. Heat oil in a large skillet; add coated fish. Turning once, pan-fry fish 3 to 4 minutes on each side until browned and fish tests done. Arrange fish on a platter; keep warm by covering with foil. Add garlic to skillet; sauté 1 minute. Add rosemary, vinegar, water and sugar. Stirring and scraping up bits from skillet, cook sauce until slightly reduced. Spoon sauce over fish; serve immediately. Makes 4 servings.

Fish & Chips

Trout Meunière with Pecans

An elegant presentation—and no bones. It's butterflied.

4 (8-oz.) trout, cleaned, or
   4 (6- to 8-oz.) fresh-water perch,
   scaled, cleaned
1/2 cup milk
1/2 cup all-purpose flour
Salt
White pepper

3 tablespoons vegetable oil
5 tablespoons butter or margarine
1/2 cup pecan halves or
   coarsely chopped pecans
3 tablespoons lemon juice
Finely slivered peel from 1 large lemon
2 tablespoons finely chopped parsley

Bone and butterfly fish, opposite, or purchase boned, butterflied fish. Rinse butterflied fish; pat dry with paper towels. Pour milk and flour into separate shallow dishes. Dip rinsed fish in milk, then dip outside of fish in flour to coat. Shake off excess flour. Season with salt and white pepper. Heat oil and 1 tablespoon butter or margarine in a large skillet. Add coated fish; pan-fry 2 to 4 minutes on each side or until golden and fish tests done. Remove cooked fish from pan; drain on paper towels. Pour fat from skillet; wipe skillet with paper towels. Melt remaining 1/4 cup butter or margarine in skillet. Add pecans; sauté 3 minutes over medium-high heat or until lightly toasted. Stir in lemon juice and lemon peel. Arrange cooked fish on a platter. Pour pecan-butter sauce over top; garnish with parsley. Makes 4 servings.

Arkansas Crispy Catfish

Serve catfish Southern-style with coleslaw and hush puppies.

12 bacon slices
6 small catfish, cleaned, skinned,
   or 5 to 7 skinless catfish fillets
Salt and pepper
1 cup all-purpose flour

1/4 cup yellow cornmeal
1 teaspoon paprika
1 egg
1/2 cup milk
6 lemon wedges

In a large skillet, fry bacon until crisp. Drain on paper towels. Pour off excess drippings, leaving 2 to 3 tablespoons in pan. Rinse fish; pat dry with paper towels. Season with salt and pepper. In a wide shallow bowl, combine flour, cornmeal and paprika. In another shallow bowl, beat together egg and milk. Dip seasoned fillets in milk mixture, then in a flour mixture. Heat bacon drippings in skillet. Pan-fry fish in hot bacon drippings 3 to 4 minutes on each side until browned and fish tests done. Serve with crisp bacon slices and lemon wedges. Makes 6 servings.

How to Bone & Butterfly Roundfish

1/Use kitchen shears or scissors to cut ribs away from flesh at stomach opening.

2/Use a boning knife to cut flesh away from ribs and backbone. From head end, pull out backbone and ribs.

Scrod with Mustard-Caper Sauce

Young cod and haddock weighing less than 2-1/2 pounds are called scrod.

4 (4- to 5-oz.) skinless scrod or about
   1-1/4 lbs. cod or haddock fillets
Salt
Freshly ground pepper
About 1/4 cup all-purpose flour
6 tablespoons butter or margarine

1 small shallot or white portion of
   green onion, finely chopped
1/2 cup dry vermouth
1-1/2 tablespoons drained capers
2 teaspoons Dijon-style mustard
1/2 cup whipping cream

Preheat oven to 165F (75C). Cut large fillets into 4 serving pieces. Rinse; pat dry with paper towels. Season with salt and pepper; dust with flour. Melt 1/4 cup butter or margarine in a large skillet over medium heat. Add coated fillets; pan-fry 1-1/2 to 3 minutes on each side or until fish tests done. Arrange cooked fillets on a platter; keep warm in oven. Discard butter or margarine from skillet. Melt remaining 2 tablespoons butter or margarine in skillet. Add shallot or green onion; sauté 1 minute or until soft and transparent. Add vermouth, capers and mustard. Stir to loosen any bits from bottom of skillet. Boil 2 to 3 minutes. Add cream; stirring frequently, cook over medium-high heat until sauce reduces and thickens enough to coat a spoon lightly. Spoon sauce over fillets. Makes 4 servings.

Rocky Mountain Trout

Enjoy this treat by a stream or recreate the river-outing atmosphere in your home.

1/2 lb. bacon slices
2 white onions, thinly sliced,
   separated into rings
1/3 cup yellow cornmeal

1/3 cup all-purpose flour
1 teaspoon salt
1/4 teaspoon pepper
4 (8-oz.) trout, cleaned, scaled

In a large skillet, fry bacon until crisp. Remove bacon from skillet; drain on paper towels. Crumble into large pieces. Reserve 2 tablespoons bacon drippings in skillet. Reserve remaining drippings. Add onion rings to drippings in skillet; sauté until soft and transparent. Remove from skillet; set aside. Add 2 to 3 tablespoons reserved drippings to skillet; heat. In a shallow dish, combine cornmeal, flour, salt and pepper. Rinse trout; shake dry. Dip rinsed trout in cornmeal mixture, thoroughly coating both sides. Pan-fry coated trout in hot bacon drippings 6 to 8 minutes, turning once, until coating is crisp and fish tests done. Spoon sautéed onions and crumbled bacon around fish. Serve immediately from skillet. If skillet is too small to fry 4 fish, pan-fry 2 fish at a time. Keep cooked fish warm by covering with foil. Makes 4 servings.

Red Snapper Veracruz

Prepare and freeze this sauce in quantity. It's good with any firm-texture fish.

1 fresh or canned jalapeño chili,
   more if desired
3 tablespoons vegetable oil
1 medium onion, chopped
3 garlic cloves, minced
1 (16-oz.) can whole peeled tomatoes,
   undrained, coarsely chopped
1/4 teaspoon salt
1/4 to 1/2 teaspoon sugar
1/4 teaspoon ground cinnamon
1/8 teaspoon ground cloves

1 tablespoon lime juice
1/3 cup small whole green olives or
   pimiento-stuffed olives
2 teaspoons capers
Salt and pepper
1-1/2 to 2 lbs. skinless red snapper,
   rock cod, pike, drum or croaker fillets
About 1/4 cup all-purpose flour
4 to 6 lime wedges
1 avocado, sliced, if desired
Cilantro or parsley sprigs, if desired

To handle fresh chili, cover your hands with rubber or plastic gloves; after handling, do not touch your face or eyes. Cut jalapeño chili into thin slivers; discard seeds. Heat 1 tablespoon oil in a medium saucepan or skillet. Add onion and garlic; sauté until onion is soft and transparent. Add jalapeño strips, tomatoes with juice, 1/4 teaspoon salt, sugar, cinnamon, cloves and lime juice. Cover; simmer 10 minutes. Stir in olives and capers. Add salt and pepper to taste; set aside. Cut fillets in 4 to 6 servings. Rinse fillets; pat dry with paper towels. Season with salt and pepper; dust with flour. Heat remaining 2 tablespoons oil in a large skillet. Add seasoned fillets; turning once, pan-fry 4 to 6 minutes or until fish tests done. Arrange on a platter. Reheat sauce, if necessary; spoon sauce over cooked fillets. Garnish with lime wedges, avocado and cilantro or parsley, if desired. Makes 4 to 6 servings.

Salmon Patties

A terrific Saturday-night-supper dish using leftover cooked salmon or canned salmon.

Dill Sauce, see below
1 (15-1/2-oz.) can salmon, drained,
   or 1 lb. leftover cooked salmon
2 cups loosely packed soft breadcrumbs
1/3 cup finely chopped green onions
1/4 cup milk
2 eggs, slightly beaten
2 tablespoons finely chopped parsley

2 tablespoons lemon juice
1/4 teaspoon salt
Pinch of pepper
1/4 teaspoon dill weed
1/2 cup cracker crumbs or
   fine dry breadcrumbs
3 tablespoons butter or margarine

Dill Sauce:
1/4 cup dairy sour cream
1/4 cup Mayonnaise, page 144,
   or other mayonnaise

1/2 teaspoon dill weed
1-1/2 teaspoons lemon juice

Prepare Dill Sauce. Separate salmon into fine flakes. In a large bowl, combine flaked salmon, soft breadcrumbs, green onions, milk, eggs, parsley, lemon juice, salt, pepper and dill weed. Shape into 8 patties, about 3/4 inch thick. Dip patties in cracker crumbs or dry breadcrumbs to coat. Melt butter or margarine in a large skillet. Pan-fry patties on both sides until golden brown. If necessary, pan-fry 4 patties at a time. Keep cooked patties warm by covering with foil. Arrange cooked salmon patties on a platter. Serve with Dill Sauce. Makes 8 patties.

Dill Sauce:
Combine all ingredients in a small bowl; stir until blended. Makes 1/2 cup.

Fried Marinated Smelt

Eat small smelt, bones and all. Bone larger smelt at the table, if desired.

1/3 cup red-wine vinegar
3 tablespoons water
2 large garlic cloves, minced
1 tablespoon minced or grated onion
1 bay leaf
3/4 teaspoon finely chopped oregano or
   1/4 teaspoon dried leaf oregano

1/4 teaspoon ground cumin
1/8 teaspoon freshly ground pepper
1 lb. small smelt, cleaned
Salt
2 to 4 tablespoons all-purpose flour
Vegetable oil for deep-frying
Lime wedges

In a heavy plastic food-storage bag, combine vinegar, water, garlic, onion, bay leaf, oregano, cumin and pepper. Rinse smelt; pat dry with paper towels. Place smelt in bag with marinade, turning to coat. Close bag; refrigerate 4 hours or longer, turning occasionally. Drain; remove and discard bay leaf. Bring smelt to room temperature. Season smelt with salt to taste; coat with flour. In a wok, deep-fat fryer or heavy saucepan, heat oil to 360F (180C) or until a 1-inch cube of bread turns golden brown in 1 minute. Fry 5 to 6 coated smelt at a time, until browned and crisp. Drain on paper towels. Serve with lime wedges. Makes about 4 servings.

Kona Coast Mahi Mahi

Thick, meat-like fillets hold their shape well in this dish.

Lime-Ginger-Butter Sauce, page 148
1-1/4 to 1-1/2 lbs. mahi mahi, sea bass,
   halibut, perch, Pacific barracuda or
   other fish fillets
Salt and pepper
About 1/4 cup all-purpose flour

3/4 cup macadamia nuts, finely chopped
1 egg
1 tablespoon water
2 tablespoons butter or margarine
2 tablespoons vegetable oil
4 lime slices

Prepare Lime-Ginger-Butter Sauce; set aside. Rinse fish; pat dry with paper towels. Cut fish into 4 equal portions. Season with salt and pepper. Lightly coat with flour; gently shake off excess flour. Pour nuts into a shallow dish. In another shallow dish, beat together egg and water. Dip flour-coated fish in egg mixture, then roll in nuts until evenly coated on both sides. Heat butter or margarine and oil in a large skillet. Add fillets; over medium-high heat, pan-fry 3 to 4 minutes on each side until outside is browned and fish tests done. Arrange on a platter. Serve with Lime-Ginger-Butter Sauce. Garnish with lime slices. Makes 4 servings.

Tempura

Also use this batter to coat assorted raw vegetables. Cook them before you cook the seafood.

Tempura Sauce, see below
1 lb. seafood, any combination:
   medium shrimp, shelled, deveined
   scallops, cut in half
   fish fillets, 1/4 inch thick,
    1/2 to 1 inch wide,
    2 to 3 inches long

1 cup all-purpose flour
1/2 teaspoon salt
2 teaspoons baking powder
1 cup water
Peanut oil for deep-frying

Tempura Sauce:
1/3 cup water
1/4 cup chicken broth
3 tablespoons soy sauce

1 teaspoon sugar
1 to 2 tablespoons dry sherry, if desired

Prepare Tempura Sauce; set aside. If serving shrimp, butterfly shrimp. Pat seafood dry with paper towels; set aside. In a medium bowl, combine flour, salt and baking powder. Gradually stir in water; batter will be lumpy. In a wok, deep-fat fryer or heavy saucepan, heat oil to 365F (185C) or until a 1-inch cube of bread turns golden brown in 1 minute. Dip seafood into batter, coating completely; let excess batter drip back into bowl. Carefully lower seafood into hot oil. Cook several pieces at a time without crowding. Fry 1 to 3 minutes, turning occasionally, until lightly browned and crisp. Drain on paper towels. Serve with Tempura Sauce. Makes 4 servings.

Tempura Sauce:
In a small saucepan, combine water, chicken broth, soy sauce, sugar and sherry, if desired. Stir sauce over medium heat until sugar dissolves. Keep warm until served. Makes about 3/4 cup.

Scallops Marsala

The aromatic flavor of Marsala complements delicately flavored scallops.

1-1/2 lbs. scallops
3 tablespoons butter or margarine
2 tablespoons finely chopped shallots or
    white portions of green onions
1/2 lb. small mushrooms, sliced

3/4 cup whipping cream
3 to 4 tablespoons Marsala or Madeira wine
Salt
White pepper
Finely chopped chervil or parsley

Cut large scallops in half horizontally. Melt half of butter or margarine in a large skillet. Add shallots or green onions and mushrooms; sauté about 3 minutes over medium-high heat. Spoon into a medium bowl; set aside. Melt remaining butter or margarine in skillet. Add scallops; sauté 1 to 2 minutes or until scallops are opaque. Do not overcook. Use a slotted spoon to add scallops to mushroom mixture; set aside. Add cream and wine to liquid in skillet; add liquid from cooked scallops and mushrooms. Cook over medium-high heat until sauce reduces to 2/3 to 3/4 cup and thickens enough to coat a spoon lightly. Add reserved mushroom mixture and scallops; heat through. Season with salt and white pepper to taste. Makes 6 main-dish or 8 appetizer servings.

Shrimp with Tomatoes & Feta Cheese

Serve this Greek-style dish from the skillet with crusty French bread and a green salad.

1/4 cup olive oil
1/2 cup chopped onions
2 garlic cloves, minced
4 medium tomatoes, peeled, seeded, chopped,
    or 2 (16-oz.) cans whole peeled
    tomatoes, drained, chopped
1/2 cup dry white or red wine
1/4 teaspoon sugar

1-1/2 teaspoons each minced oregano,
    basil and thyme or 1/2 teaspoon each
    dried leaf oregano, basil and thyme
2 tablespoons finely chopped parsley
1-1/2 lbs. medium shrimp, shelled, deveined
1/4 lb. feta cheese, cut in 1/4-inch cubes
12 Greek or Italian olives
Salt and pepper

Heat oil in a large skillet. Add onions and garlic; sauté until onions are soft and transparent. Add tomatoes, wine, sugar, oregano, basil, thyme and 1 tablespoon parsley. Cook over medium-high heat 3 to 5 minutes, stirring frequently, until sauce is reduced slightly. Reduce heat to medium. Rinse shrimp; pat dry with paper towels. Add rinsed shrimp to onion mixture. Cook 3 to 5 minutes or until shrimp become firm and turn pink. Remove skillet from heat. Gently stir in cheese and olives. Season with salt and pepper to taste. Serve from skillet or spoon into a serving bowl. Sprinkle with remaining parsley. Makes 4 to 6 servings.

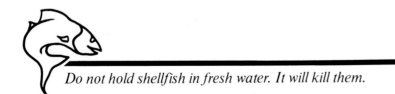

Do not hold shellfish in fresh water. It will kill them.

How to Make Scallops Marsala

1/Sauté scallops 1 to 2 minutes or until opaque. Do not overcook.

2/Cook sauce until reduced and thick enough to coat a spoon lightly.

Garlic Shrimp

The subtle touch of anise-flavored liqueur adds an interesting flavor.

1/2 cup butter or margarine,
  room temperature
4 garlic cloves, minced
2 tablespoons finely chopped parsley
1-1/2 tablespoons finely chopped shallots
1/4 teaspoon paprika
1/8 teaspoon red (cayenne) pepper
2 to 3 teaspoons Pernod or
  other anise-flavored liqueur

1-1/2 lbs. medium or large shrimp,
  shelled, deveined
About 1/4 cup all-purpose flour
1/3 cup olive oil
2 tablespoons lemon juice
3/4 cup dry white wine
Salt and black pepper
Chopped parsley, if desired

In a small bowl, cream together butter or margarine, garlic, 2 tablespoons parsley, shallots, paprika, red pepper and liqueur. Lightly dust shrimp with flour. Heat oil in a large skillet. Add shrimp; stirring frequently, pan-fry over medium heat 3 to 4 minutes or until shrimp become firm and turn pink. Drain off oil. Add lemon juice and wine to shrimp. Shake pan over medium-high heat about 30 seconds. Add garlic mixture. Stir and toss shrimp until butter melts and mixture coats shrimp. Season with salt and black pepper to taste. Spoon onto a platter. Sprinkle with chopped parsley; serve immediately. Makes 6 servings.

Fried Chinese Shrimp Balls

Serve this marvelous hot appetizer at your next party.

Orange-Soy Dipping Sauce, see below
1 lb. medium to large shrimp,
　shelled, deveined
1 (8-oz.) can water chestnuts, drained
1 egg
1 green onion, finely chopped
1-1/2 tablespoons cornstarch

1 teaspoon finely shredded gingerroot or
　1/4 teaspoon ground ginger
1/2 teaspoon salt
Pinch of white pepper
1 teaspoon sesame oil, if desired
Vegetable oil for deep-frying
Chinese hot mustard

Orange-Soy Dipping Sauce:
1/2 cup orange marmalade
1 tablespoon soy sauce
1 teaspoon prepared horseradish

1 teaspoon lemon juice
1/8 teaspoon red (cayenne) pepper
1/4 teaspoon sesame oil, if desired

Prepare Orange-Soy Dipping Sauce; set aside. Finely chop shrimp and water chestnuts. In a medium bowl, lightly beat egg. Stir in chopped shrimp and water chestnuts, green onion, cornstarch, gingerroot or ground ginger, salt, white pepper and sesame oil, if desired. Shape mixture into 1-inch balls. Preheat oven to 165F (75C). In a wok, deep-fat fryer or heavy saucepan, heat oil to 365F (185C) or until a 1-inch cube of bread turns golden brown in 1 minute. Fry 6 to 8 shrimp balls at a time in hot oil. Cook 40 to 60 seconds or until golden brown, turning 2 or 3 times. Drain on paper towels; keep hot in oven. Pour mustard and Orange-Soy Dipping Sauce into separate bowls. Arrange cooked shrimp balls on a platter or in a serving bowl. Serve with bamboo skewers or wooden picks for dipping balls into mustard and sauce. Makes about 30 shrimp balls.

Orange-Soy Dipping Sauce: Photo on page 151.
In a small bowl, combine all ingredients. Stir to blend. Makes about 1/2 cup.

Garlic Squid Sauté

Distinctly garlic-flavored, easy to make and inexpensive.

3 lbs. squid
3 tablespoons olive oil
2 tablespoons butter or margarine
5 or 6 garlic cloves, minced
1 cup chopped parsley

2 to 3 tablespoons lemon juice
Salt
Freshly ground pepper
Freshly grated Parmesan cheese,
　if desired

Clean squid. Cut bodies of squid into 1/2- to 3/4-inch crosswise slices. Trim long tentacles; cut tentacles crosswise in halves or quarters. Heat olive oil and butter or margarine in a large skillet. Add squid pieces; sauté 1 to 1-1/2 minutes over medium-high heat. After 30 seconds, stir in garlic, parsley and lemon juice. Season with salt and pepper to taste. Spoon onto a platter. If desired, serve Parmesan cheese separately. Makes 4 to 6 servings.

Pan-Fried Abalone Steaks

The secret to preparing abalone is to cook it simply and quickly.

8 small or 4 large fresh or
   frozen abalone steaks
6 tablespoons butter or margarine
1 to 2 tablespoons lemon or lime juice
About 1/4 cup all-purpose flour
Salt and pepper

2 eggs
2 tablespoons water
1 tablespoon vegetable oil
2 tablespoons butter or margarine
Finely chopped parsley
4 lemon wedges

Thaw frozen abalone steaks. Melt 6 tablespoons butter or margarine in a small saucepan. Add lemon or lime juice to taste. Keep warm over low heat. Pour flour into a wide shallow bowl; stir in salt and pepper to taste. In another shallow bowl, beat together eggs and water. Lightly coat abalone steaks with flour mixture; gently shake to remove excess flour. Dip in egg mixture, then dip in flour again to lightly coat. Heat oil and 2 tablespoons butter or margarine in a large skillet. Add coated abalone steaks. Pan-fry steaks 30 to 45 seconds on each side; turn once. Arrange cooked steaks on a platter; garnish with parsley. Serve with lemon wedges and warm butter sauce. Makes 4 servings.

Preparing Abalone Steaks

Using a large spoon and a knife, pry the muscular foot out of the shell, severing the muscle that connects the foot to the shell. Pull off and discard the viscera clinging to the foot. Trim off the dark covering along the edges and lower part of the foot. Use trimmings for soup. Slice steaks across the grain, about 3/8 inch thick. Pound the steaks with a mallet to tenderize.

If you don't have a deep-frying thermometer, drop a 1-inch square of bread into the hot fat. At 365F to 375F (185C to 190C), it will brown in 50 seconds.

Deep-Fried Squid

This popular restaurant appetizer is inexpensive to make at home, and perfect for parties.

Seafood Cocktail Sauce, page 153,
   if desired
2 lbs. squid
1 cup all-purpose flour
1/2 teaspoon salt

Pinch of pepper
2 eggs
2 tablespoons milk
Oil for deep-frying
Lemon wedges

Prepare Seafood Cocktail Sauce, if desired. Clean squid. Cut bodies of squid into 3/4-inch slices. Trim long tentacles; cut tentacles crosswise in halves or quarters. Dry squid pieces with paper towels. In a shallow dish, combine flour, salt and pepper. In another shallow dish, beat together eggs and milk. Preheat oven to 165F (75C). In a wok, deep-fat fryer or heavy saucepan, heat oil to 365F (185C) or until a 1-inch cube of bread turns golden brown in 1 minute. Lightly coat squid pieces with flour mixture. Dip in egg mixture, then dip in flour mixture again to lightly coat. Fry 5 or 6 pieces at a time 1 to 1-1/2 minutes or until coating is crisp and golden brown. Drain on paper towels; keep warm in oven until all are cooked. Serve with lemon wedges and Seafood Cocktail Sauce, if desired. Makes 10 to 12 appetizer servings.

Variation

Substitute 1/2 cup dry breadcrumbs for 1/2 cup flour.

Pan-Fried Oysters

The key to tasty oysters is in the preparation—pan-fry briefly to serve lightly browned.

Seafood Cocktail Sauce, page 153,
   if desired
2 (8- or 10-oz.) jars or
   20 freshly shucked oysters
Salt and pepper
1/2 cup all-purpose flour

3/4 cup fine cracker crumbs or
   dry breadcrumbs
2 eggs
2 tablespoons milk
3 to 4 tablespoons butter or margarine
Lemon wedges

Prepare Seafood Cocktail Sauce, if desired. Drain oysters; pat dry with paper towels. Sprinkle with salt and pepper. Combine flour and crumbs in a shallow bowl. In another shallow bowl, beat together eggs and milk. Dip seasoned oysters in crumb mixture. Dip in egg mixture, then in crumb mixture again, coating thoroughly. Melt butter or margarine in a large skillet. Add coated oysters; pan-fry until lightly browned on one side. Using a spatula or tongs, carefully turn and brown other side. Do not overcook. Serve with lemon wedges and Seafood Cocktail Sauce, if desired. Makes 4 to 5 servings.

Variation

Add 1 tablespoon finely chopped parsley and 1 teaspoon chopped tarragon to cracker-crumb mixture. Or, add chopped parsley or chopped tarragon to taste.

How to Make Deep-Fried Squid

1/Coat squid pieces with flour mixture. Dip in egg mixture, then coat with flour mixture again.

2/Fry 5 or 6 pieces at a time until coating is crisp and golden brown. Drain on paper towels.

Southern-Style Deep-Fried Oysters

A traditional Southern favorite. Perfect as finger-food or for a casual supper.

Seafood Cocktail Sauce, page 153,
  if desired
20 oysters, shucked, or
  2 (8- or 10-oz.) jars shucked oysters
Vegetable oil for deep-frying

Salt
Freshly ground pepper
3/4 cup yellow cornmeal
Lemon wedges or ketchup, if desired

Prepare Seafood Cocktail Sauce, if desired. Drain oysters; pat dry with paper towels. If oysters are large, cut in half; set aside. Preheat oven to 165F (75C). In a wok, deep-fat fryer or heavy saucepan, heat oil to 365F (185C) or until a 1-inch cube of bread turns golden brown in 1 minute. Season oysters with salt and pepper. Pour cornmeal into a shallow bowl. Roll seasoned oysters in cornmeal, coating completely. Fry 4 or 5 coated oysters at a time until coating is crisp and golden brown. Do not overcook; drain on paper towels. Keep warm in oven until all are cooked. Serve with Seafood Cocktail Sauce, lemon wedges or ketchup, if desired. Makes 3 main-dish or 5 appetizer servings.

Panned Soft-Shell Crab

A summer delicacy. Buy the crabs dressed or do it yourself.

8 soft-shell crab, dressed, below
1/2 cup all-purpose flour
1/2 teaspoon salt
Red (cayenne) pepper
About 6 tablespoons butter or margarine

About 2 tablespoons vegetable oil
1 to 2 tablespoons Pernod or
   other anise-flavored liqueur,
   if desired
4 lemon wedges

Preheat oven to 160F (70C). Rinse crab; pat dry with paper towels. In a shallow dish, combine flour, salt and red pepper. Melt 2 tablespoons butter or margarine in a large skillet. Add 1 tablespoon oil. Coat rinsed crab with flour mixture. When butter and oil are hot, add coated crabs, belly-side down. Over medium-high heat, pan-fry 3 to 5 minutes until browned. Turn and pan-fry 2 to 3 minutes longer. Add more butter or margarine and oil to pan if necessary during cooking. Place cooked crab on a platter. Keep warm in oven until all crab are cooked. Melt 2 tablespoon butter or margarine in skillet; add liqueur, if desired. Stir to loosen drippings; spoon sauce over cooked crab. Serve with lemon wedges. Makes 4 servings.

To Dress Soft-Shell Crab

Fish dealers will often dress soft-shell crab for you. If you must dress the crab yourself, rinse it thoroughly. Cut off the eyes with a knife or kitchen shears. Press behind where the eyes were to expose the bile sac; pull out the bile sac. Turn the crab on its back. Lift up and cut off the apron, a rough triangle of soft shell. Lift up the flaps at each side by the legs and pull out the spongy gills. Rinse the crab thoroughly; pat dry with paper towels. The whole soft-shell crab is eaten, including the shell.

Crab Sauté

Crabmeat and julienned vegetables are quickly sautéed. Excellent for the busy cook!

1/4 cup butter or margarine
1 tablespoon minced garlic
2 teaspoons finely shredded gingerroot
1-1/2 cups julienned carrots (1 lb.)
3 oz. snow peas, cut diagonally in 1/2- to
   3/4-inch pieces (about 1 cup)
3/4 cup fine julienned leeks,
   white portions only

3 slender green onions,
   cut in 1-inch diagonal pieces
3/4 lb. fresh or frozen crabmeat or
   2 (6-oz.) cans crabmeat, drained
1 to 1-1/2 tablespoons lemon juice
Salt
White pepper

Melt butter or margarine in a large skillet. Add garlic and gingerroot; sauté about 30 seconds. Add vegetables in order listed, sautéing each about 30 seconds before adding next vegetable. Add crabmeat. Season with lemon juice, salt and white pepper to taste. Serve immediately. Makes 4 to 6 servings.

How to Make Panned Soft-Shell Crab

1/Coat crab with flour mixture. Cook, belly-side down, in hot fat until browned. Turn and brown other side.

2/Stir liqueur in skillet to loosen bits from bottom. Spoon over cooked crab. Serve with lemon wedges.

Maryland Crab Cakes

Seafood seasoning and crab seasoning are available at fish and specialty-food markets.

1 egg, slightly beaten
1 cup fresh breadcrumbs
1/4 cup Mayonnaise, page 144,
 or other mayonnaise
1/4 cup finely chopped parsley
1 teaspoon Worcestershire sauce
1/2 to 1 teaspoon seafood seasoning or
 crab seasoning

1/4 teaspoon dry mustard
Pinch red (cayenne) pepper
Salt and black pepper
1 lb. crabmeat
1 to 2 tablespoons butter or margarine
1 to 2 tablespoons vegetable oil
6 lemon wedges

In a medium bowl, combine egg, 3/4 cup breadcrumbs, mayonnaise, parsley, Worcestershire sauce, seafood seasoning or crab seasoning, mustard and red pepper. Add salt and black pepper to taste. Gently fold in crabmeat. Shape mixture into 6 balls; flatten into 3-inch cakes. Coat crab cakes with remaining 1/4 cup breadcrumbs; place coated crab cakes on a platter. Cover; refrigerate 1 hour. In a large skillet, heat 1 tablespoon butter or margarine and 1 tablespoon oil. Pan-fry crab cakes 3 to 4 minutes on each side or until golden brown. Add more butter or margarine and oil to skillet as necessary. Serve with lemon wedges. Makes 6 servings.

Shad Roe with Bacon

Considered a delicacy by many, shad roe is available only 3 to 4 weeks in the spring.

4 small shad-roe sets
8 bacon slices
1 large onion, sliced, separated into rings
Salt and pepper

About 1/4 cup all-purpose flour
4 lemon wedges
Finely chopped parsley

Rinse roe thoroughly, being careful not to break membrane. In a medium bowl, soak roe 5 minutes in lightly salted ice water or until slightly firm. Meanwhile, in a large skillet, fry bacon until crisp; drain on paper towels. Pour all but 2 to 3 tablespoons bacon drippings from skillet. Add onion rings; sauté until tender. Using a slotted spoon, transfer sautéed onions to a small bowl; set aside. Drain roe; gently pat dry with paper towels. Season well with salt and pepper; lightly coat with flour. Add coated roe to skillet; cover skillet. Over medium heat, cook 3 to 5 minutes. Using a spatula, carefully turn roe. Cook, uncovered, 3 to 5 minutes longer or to desired doneness. Roe may be pink in center or may be cooked until no longer pink. Place cooked roe on a platter; garnish with cooked bacon, sautéed onions, lemon wedges and parsley. Makes 4 servings.

Roe & Caviar

True caviar is the salted *roe,* or eggs, of sturgeon. But the salted roe of salmon, whitefish, lumpfish, shad, herring, mullet, pike and perch is widely used. It is qualified by the name of the fish from which it came, such as *salmon caviar* or *lumpfish caviar.*

While sturgeon caviar is the most expensive, lumpfish caviar, exported from Iceland, is the least expensive. In their natural state, lumpfish eggs are tan. Therefore, they are usually dyed black or red. If you're using caviar as a garnish or mixed with other ingredients, lumpfish caviar is quite suitable.

Today, most sturgeon caviar is exported from Russia and Iran. There is a limited production of caviar from sturgeon caught in Oregon and Washington. Of the varieties of sturgeon that produce caviar, *beluga* is the largest, sometimes reaching up to 2500 pounds and producing 120 pounds of roe. The next largest is *osetra,* and the smallest is *sevruga.* The best caviar is prepared from sturgeon caught in the spring, when the water is cold, making the roe firm.

Roe is carefully sieved, then steeped in a salt solution. Top-quality caviar is known as *malosol,* meaning *little salt.* Beluga malosol is the *crème de la crème* of caviar. The color of sturgeon caviar, which ranges from gray to black, is not an indication of quality.

Chilled caviar tastes best. Serve sturgeon caviar in a small bowl surrounded by crushed ice, with lemon wedges, French bread or toast, and sweet butter. Chopped hard-cooked egg and minced onion are suitable accompaniments only for lesser-quality caviar. Champagne and iced vodka are traditional accompaniments with any caviar.

Roe taken from fish you catch can be cooked, as in Shad Roe with Bacon, above. Do not store roe more than one day.

Broiling & Grilling

Like baking, broiling and grilling are dry-heat cooking methods. Whole fish, fillets, steaks and chunks can be broiled or grilled. Skewered pieces, as in Fish on a Stick and Grilled Skewered Shellfish, are fun and easy to broil or grill. High-fat fish, such as mackerel, bluefish, mullet and tuna, are especially good broiled or grilled. Almost any fish can be cooked by these methods. All fish, especially lean fish, require basting with oil, melted butter or an oil-base marinade during cooking to keep them from drying out.

Broiling exposes fish to direct heat, giving an appetizing golden-brown surface. Preheat the broiler, then oil the broiling pan to prevent sticking. Adjust the pan so the fish is four to six inches from the heat—the thicker the fish, the greater the distance. Lower the broiling pan if the fish browns too quickly.

For broiling, fish should be 1/2 to 1-1/2 inches thick. Pieces under 1/2 inch thick often overcook before they brown. Pieces over 1-1/2 inches thick may char on the outside before they're done. Most fillets and steaks are only cooked on one side; thick pieces may require turning.

Grilled fish is cooked on a metal grill over direct heat. The heat source may be charcoal or wood, a gas flame or an electric heating element. When using a charcoal grill, try mesquite charcoal or hardwood. These woods impart a wonderful flavor and aroma, and burn hotter than other charcoal briquets. This is an advantage because high heat seals in natural juices and flavor.

Nearly any fish or shellfish that can be broiled can be grilled. Fish with a pronounced flavor are enhanced by a smoky barbecue flavor. This includes mackerel, bluefish, salmon, trout, tuna and fish with a meat-like texture, such as swordfish and shark. The delicate flavor of flounder and sole, however, may be overwhelmed by the smoke.

To charcoal grill, build a fire with mesquite, hardwood or charcoal briquets 30 to 40 minutes before cooking time. When the charcoal is covered with gray ash, spread the coals in a single layer. Set an oiled grill 4 to 6 inches above the coals. Let the grill get hot before adding fish.

To prevent sticking on any grill, generously oil the fish, unless it was marinated in an oil-base marinade. Clean the grill each time it is used. Charred bits of food from previous grillings cause sticking.

To turn fish easily and help prevent sticking, cook whole fish in a fish-shape, hinged, wire basket. Grill fillets and steaks in a flat, rectangular grill similar to an old-fashion toaster grill. Or, make loops from foil and use to turn fish as suggested with Charcoal-Grilled Mackerel. To keep soft-texture fillets, such as sablefish, from breaking up and falling through the grill, place a piece of greased foil directly on the grill. With a skewer, poke holes in the foil. The holes let fat drain and let smoke and heat penetrate the fillets, cooking and flavoring them.

Fish on a Stick

This is a fun way to handle fillets on the grill.

1/2 to 1 teaspoon finely
   shredded orange peel
1/3 cup fresh orange juice
2 tablespoons peanut oil or vegetable oil
2 tablespoons soy sauce
1 tablespoon cider vinegar
1 tablespoon sugar

1 to 2 teaspoons finely shredded gingerroot or
   1/4 teaspoon ground ginger
2 teaspoons sesame oil, if desired
1-1/4 to 1-1/2 lbs. sturgeon, cod or
   other firm-texture skinless fillets,
   about 1 inch thick
Cooked rice, if desired

In a plastic food-storage bag, combine orange peel, orange juice, peanut or vegetable oil, soy sauce, vinegar, sugar, gingerroot or ground ginger and sesame oil, if desired; set aside. Cut fillets lengthwise into 8 strips. Place strips in bag with marinade; close bag. Refrigerate at least 30 minutes. Preheat grill; grease rack. Remove fish strips from marinade; reserve marinade. Thread fish strips on metal skewers, weaving in and out at 2- to 3-inch intervals. Place skewered fish on greased rack 4 to 6 inches above hot coals or high heat. Basting with reserved marinade and turning skewers once or twice, grill 7 to 8 minutes or until fish tests done. Serve with cooked rice, if desired. Makes 4 servings.

Variation

Marinated fish strips may be broiled. Place skewered fish on a greased broiling pan about 4 inches from heat. Basting with reserved marinade, broil 7 to 8 minutes or until fish tests done; turn skewers after 4 minutes.

How to Make Fish on a Stick

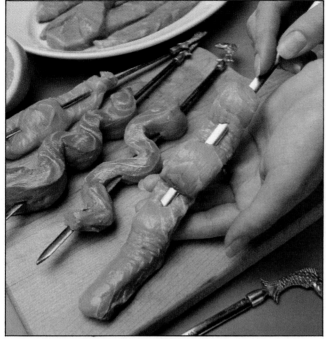

1/Thread marinated fish strips on metal skewers, weaving in and out at 2- to 3-inch intervals.

2/Grill on greased rack until fish tests done. Serve with cooked rice, if desired.

Oregon Salmon

The tasty topping puffs and browns under the broiler.

6 salmon steaks, 3/4 inch thick
1 tablespoon lemon juice
Salt and black pepper
2 egg whites
3/4 cup Mayonnaise, page 144,
   or other mayonnaise
1/2 cup finely shredded Gruyère or
   Cheddar cheese (2 oz.)

1/4 cup chopped green onions
2 tablespoons finely chopped parsley
1 tablespoon finely chopped dill or
   1 teaspoon dill weed
Pinch of red (cayenne) pepper

Preheat broiler. Generously grease a broiling pan. Arrange salmon steaks on greased pan. Sprinkle with lemon juice; season lightly with salt and black pepper. Broil 4 to 6 inches from heat, 6 to 8 minutes or until fish tests done. Meanwhile, in a medium bowl, beat egg whites until stiff but not dry. Fold in mayonnaise, cheese, green onions, parsley, dill, pinch of salt and red pepper. Spread mixture evenly over fish; broil until lightly browned. Makes 6 servings.

Fish Fleming

Fresh mint complements the barbecue flavor.

4 (5- to 7-oz.) swordfish or other
   firm-texture fish steaks
Salt and pepper
1/4 cup butter or margarine

2 small garlic cloves, minced
2 tablespoons finely chopped mint
2 teaspoons lemon juice
Mint sprigs, if desired

Preheat grill; grease rack. Rinse fish; pat dry with paper towels. Season with salt and pepper. Melt butter or margarine in a small saucepan. Add garlic, chopped mint and lemon juice. Spoon garlic mixture over seasoned fish. Place on greased rack 3 to 4 inches above hot coals or high heat. Turning once and basting 2 or 3 times with garlic mixture, grill 5 to 8 minutes or until fish tests done. Spoon any remaining garlic mixture over cooked fish or on platter; place fish on platter. Garnish with mint sprigs, if desired. Makes 4 servings.

Variation

Substitute 3/4-inch-thick firm-texture fillets for fish steaks.

Grilled Yellowfin Tuna

These steaks have the best flavor when eaten rare.

Tomato-Basil-Butter Sauce, see below
6 (5- to 7-oz.) yellowfin tuna or
   other red-flesh tuna steaks,
   about 1 inch thick

Salt and pepper
Olive oil

Tomato-Basil-Butter Sauce:
1-1/2 tablespoons butter
3 small tomatoes, peeled, seeded, chopped
1/8 teaspoon sugar
1/4 cup butter, room temperature

1 small garlic clove, minced
1 tablespoon finely chopped basil,
   or to taste
Salt and pepper

Preheat grill; grease rack. Prepare Tomato-Basil-Butter Sauce. Rinse tuna; pat dry with paper towels. Season rinsed tuna with salt and pepper. Brush with olive oil. Place on greased rack about 4 inches above hot coals or high heat. Grill 1 to 2 minutes on each side, turning once. *Do not cook well-done.* Fish should remain rare and red in center. Serve with Tomato-Basil-Butter Sauce. Makes 6 servings.

Tomato-Basil-Butter Sauce:

Melt 1-1/2 tablespoons butter in a small skillet. Add tomatoes and sugar. Stirring frequently, cook until liquid evaporates and mixture thickens. Add 1/4 cup butter and garlic. Stir over medium heat until mixture develops a sauce-like consistency. Stir in 1 tablespoon or more basil. Add salt and pepper to taste. Makes 2/3 cup.

Note: This recipe is not suitable for grilling in a hinged wire basket.

Grilled Whole Fish

Barbecuing fish is fun and easy.

**Lemon-Parsley Butter or
    Mustard Butter, page 156**
**1 (2-1/2- to 3-1/2-lb.) whole fish,
    cleaned, scaled**
Salt and pepper

**10 to 15 thyme sprigs or
    2 to 3 teaspoons dried leaf thyme**
Vegetable oil
Lemon wedges

Prepare Lemon-Parsley Butter or Mustard Butter; set aside. Preheat grill; grease rack or a hinged wire basket. Remove head and tail from fish, if desired. Rinse fish inside and out; pat dry with paper towels. Season inside and out with salt and pepper. Place thyme sprigs or sprinkle dried thyme inside seasoned fish. Generously rub outside of fish with oil. Cook fish on rack or in hinged wire basket. *To cook on grill,* tear off 2 (12-inch) strips heavy foil. Fold each strip in half lengthwise, 4 times. Grease one side of strips. Place 1 strip under each end of fish. Fold strips around fish, twisting at belly to make handles for turning fish. Place fish on greased rack, 4 to 6 inches above hot coals or high heat. *To cook fish in a hinged wire basket,* place fish in greased basket. Basket has legs; therefore, regular wire rack may be removed from grill. Place basket so fish is 4 inches above hot coals. Cover barbecue with lid or foil; cut 2 slits in center of foil for vents. Or, cover fish with a tent of heavy foil. Grill 5 to 8 minutes; remove lid or foil covering. Wearing oven mitts, turn fish by grasping twisted portions of foil bands. If fish is in metal basket, turn basket over. Cover and cook 5 to 8 minutes longer or until fish tests done. Place cooked fish on a platter. Remove foil bands, if used. Serve with Lemon-Parsley Butter or Mustard Butter and lemon wedges. Makes 4 to 6 servings.

Grilled Fillets

Serve with a tart sauce, such as Fresh Mexican Salsa, page 148, or Italian Salsa Verde, page 150.

**1-1/2 lbs. bluefish, mullet or
    mackerel fillets**
Salt and pepper

Vegetable oil
Lime or lemon wedges

Preheat grill; grease rack or a hinged wire basket. Rinse fillets; pat dry with paper towels. Cut rinsed fillets into 4 serving pieces. Season with salt and pepper. Generously rub seasoned fillets with oil. *To grill fillets on rack,* place oiled fish on greased rack, skin-side up, 4 to 6 inches above hot coals or high heat. *To grill in hinged wire basket,* place oiled fish in greased basket. Basket has legs; therefore, regular wire rack may be removed from grill. Place basket so fillets are 4 to 6 inches above hot coals or high heat. Grill fish on rack or in basket 3 to 4 minutes. Turn; grill 2 to 4 minutes longer or until fish tests done. Place grilled fillets on a platter. Serve with lime or lemon wedges. Makes 4 servings.

Note: To remove dark flesh strip from bluefish fillet, see page 12.

How to Grill Whole Fish

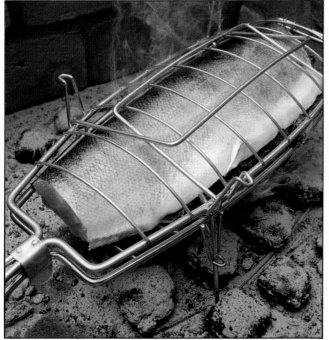

1/Place fish in hinged wire basket or rack. Grill about 4 inches above coals. Grasp handle to turn.

2/Or, place a foil strip under each end of fish. Twist foil strips at belly opening to make handles for turning.

Grilled Steaks with Salsa

Fresh salsa adds color and a piquant flavor to grilled fish steaks.

Fresh Mexican Salsa, page 148
2 garlic cloves, minced
1-1/2 teaspoons finely chopped oregano or
   1/2 teaspoon dried leaf oregano
1 teaspoon salt

2 tablespoons lime juice
1/3 cup olive oil
4 (5- to 8-oz.) albacore, bonito,
   swordfish or shark steaks

Prepare Fresh Mexican Salsa; set aside. In a small bowl, combine garlic, oregano and salt. Beat in lime juice, then olive oil. Rinse fish steaks; pat dry with paper towels. Rub garlic mixture into rinsed steaks. Let stand at room temperature while preheating grill; grease rack or hinged wire basket. Place coated steaks on greased rack or in greased basket; place 4 to 6 inches above hot coals or high heat. Turning once, grill 7 to 10 minutes or until fish tests done. Serve with Fresh Mexican Salsa. Makes 4 servings.

Albacore, also called white *or* white-meat tuna, *is the finest tuna canned. Light or light-meat tuna comes from other varieties of tuna.*

Grilled Lobster Tails

Want to prepare a special treat? Make barbecued or broiled lobster tails.

Lemon-Garlic-Butter Sauce, page 155,	**4 (1/2-lb.) lobster tails**
or 1/2 cup butter or margarine, melted	**Lemon wedges**

Prepare Lemon-Garlic-Butter Sauce; keep melted. Preheat grill. To prepare lobster, cut along edges of tail undershells with kitchen shears. Clip off fins along outer edges. Peel back and discard soft undershell. Bend tail backward, cracking several joints in overshell to prevent curling. Brush lobster with Lemon-Garlic-Butter Sauce or butter or margarine. Grease rack; place lobster, shell-side down, on greased rack 4 to 6 inches above hot coals or high heat. Cover grill with lid or foil; cut 2 slits in center of foil for vents. Or, cover lobster with a tent of heavy foil. Grill 5 minutes. Brush again with sauce or butter or margarine. Turn lobster. Cover and cook 3 to 5 minutes longer or until flesh is opaque. Serve with remaining sauce or butter or margarine. Garnish with lemon wedges. Makes 4 servings.

Variation

To oven-broil lobster, prepare as directed above. Broil 4 to 6 inches from heat. Serve as above.

Charcoal-Grilled Mackerel

Fish are easy to turn on the grill when you use Reynolds easy-to-make foil strips.

1 (3- to 3-1/2-lb.) Spanish mackerel,	**1 tablespoon finely chopped oregano or**
cleaned, scaled, or	**1 teaspoon dried leaf oregano**
4 (1/2- to 1-lb.) mackerel,	**1-1/2 teaspoons chopped rosemary or**
cleaned, scaled	**3/4 teaspoon dried leaf rosemary**
Salt and pepper	**1/4 cup olive oil**
1/3 cup lemon juice	**2 to 8 bacon slices**
2 garlic cloves, minced	**Lemon wedges**

Preheat grill; grease rack. Remove fish heads and tails, if desired. Rinse fish inside and out; pat dry with paper towels. Season inside and out with salt and pepper. Make 3 shallow diagonal cuts on each side of seasoned fish. In a small bowl, combine lemon juice, garlic, oregano and rosemary. Beat in olive oil. Brush fish inside and out with lemon-oil mixture. Lay 1 bacon slice lengthwise on both side of each fish. Tear off 2 (12-inch) strips heavy foil for each fish. Fold each strip in half lengthwise, 4 times. Grease one side of strips. Place 1 strip under each end of fish. Fold strips around fish, twisting at belly to secure bacon and make handles for turning fish. Place fish on greased rack 4 to 6 inches above hot coals or high heat. Cover barbecue with a lid or foil; cut 2 slits in center of foil for vents. Or, cover fish with a tent of heavy foil. Grill large fish 6 to 8 minutes on each side and small fish 3 to 5 minutes on each side or until fish tests done. Remove lid or foil covering. Wearing oven mitts, turn fish by grasping twisted portions of foil bands. Place cooked fish on a platter; remove foil loops. Serve with lemon wedges. Makes 4 servings.

How to Make Grilled Lobster Tails

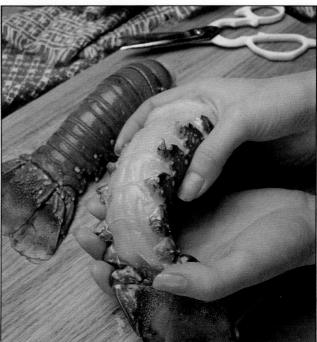

1/Using kitchen shears, cut along edges of undershell; cut off fins along sides.

2/Discard soft undershell. Bend tail back, cracking joints in overshell. Barbecue as directed.

Broiled Salmon McCole

A winner—easy, fast, eye-appealing and delicious.

1-1/2 to 2 lbs. skinless salmon fillets or
   other skinless firm-texture
   fish fillets
1/2 cup butter or margarine
3 to 4 tablespoons prepared
   whole-seed mustard

2 tablespoons finely chopped shallots
   or onion
1 tablespoon lemon juice
1 teaspoon paprika
Pinch of red (cayenne) pepper
Salt

Purchase 6 individual fillets or cut large fillets into 6 servings. Preheat broiler. Grease a broiling pan; place fillets on greased pan. Melt butter or margarine in a small saucepan. Stir in mustard, shallots or onion, lemon juice, paprika and red pepper. Add salt to taste. Spoon mustard sauce evenly over fillets. Broil 4 to 6 inches from heat, 4 to 6 minutes or until fish tests done and top coating is browned. Makes 6 servings.

Barbecued Shrimp

Great finger-food as well as main-dish fare.

2 tablespoons butter or margarine
1/2 cup chopped onion
3/4 cup ketchup
1/4 cup water
2-1/2 tablespoons Worcestershire sauce
3 tablespoons brown sugar
1 tablespoon white vinegar

1 tablespoon tomato paste
1/2 teaspoon dry mustard
Dash of red (cayenne) pepper
24 large or jumbo shrimp,
   shelled, deveined
12 bacon slices, cut in halves

Melt butter or margarine in a medium saucepan. Add onion; sauté until soft and transparent. Stir in ketchup, water, Worcestershire sauce, brown sugar, vinegar, tomato paste, dry mustard and red pepper. Stirring occasionally, simmer uncovered 15 minutes. Remove from heat. Immediately stir shrimp into sauce, covering completely. Let stand 15 minutes. Preheat broiler or grill; grease rack. Remove shrimp from sauce. Wrap each coated shrimp in a piece of bacon; secure with a wooden pick. If desired, thread 4 or 5 bacon-wrapped shrimp on a skewer. Place on greased rack about 4 inches from hot coals or high heat. Cook 3 to 4 minutes. Turn; cook remaining side until bacon is crisp. Reheat sauce; serve separately. Makes 5 or 6 main-dish servings or 8 to 12 appetizer servings.

Barbecued Oysters or Clams

These charcoal-grilled mollusks are hard to beat for good eating.

24 oysters, clams or a combination
1 cup butter or margarine
1 teaspoon Worcestershire sauce

1 teaspoon lemon juice, or to taste
1 large garlic clove, minced
3 or 4 drops hot-pepper sauce

Preheat grill. Scrub oysters or clams with a brush to remove sand from shells. Discard oysters or clams that stay open. Melt butter or margarine in a small saucepan. Add Worcestershire sauce, lemon juice, garlic and hot-pepper sauce. Keep sauce hot on grill, if desired. Place cleaned oysters or clams on rack 2 to 4 inches above hot coals or high heat. Grill until shells open; discard shells that do not open. Use your fingers to finish opening shells. Serve with butter sauce. Makes 3 to 4 servings.

Barbecued Shrimp

Easy Broiled Fish

Sometimes the simplest fish dishes are the best.

4 (5- to 7-oz.) firm-texture fish steaks or
  skinless fillets,
    about 3/4 inch thick
Salt and pepper

1/4 to 1/3 cup Mayonnaise, page 144,
  or other mayonnaise
2 tablespoons freshly grated Parmesan cheese

Preheat broiler. Rinse steaks or fillets; pat dry with paper towels. Season with salt and pepper. Spread 1 to 1-1/2 tablespoons mayonnaise over top of each steak or fillet. Sprinkle 1-1/2 teaspoons cheese on top of each. Place on broiling pan. Broil 4 to 6 inches from heat, 5 to 8 minutes or until top is puffed and brown, and fish tests done. Makes 4 servings.

Grilled Skewered Shellfish

If the weather is too blustery to barbecue, broil these kabobs.

Lemon-Garlic-Butter Sauce or
  Lime-Butter Sauce, page 155
4 medium squid, cleaned
24 medium shrimp

24 scallops
24 cherry tomatoes
24 mushrooms
1 large red onion, cut in 12 pieces

Preheat grill; grease rack. Prepare Lemon-Garlic-Butter Sauce or Lime-Butter Sauce. Cut body of squid in 1-inch slices. On 12 metal skewers, thread squid pieces alternately with shrimp, scallops, tomatoes, mushrooms and onion pieces. Place on greased rack 4 to 6 inches above hot coals or high heat; generously brush with butter sauce. Basting with butter sauce and turning skewers once or twice, grill 5 to 10 minutes or until shrimp become firm and turn pink. Makes 6 servings.

Broiled Alaskan King-Crab Legs

Frozen king-crab legs are available in most supermarkets.

1 (10- to 12-oz.) pkg. frozen, split,
  cooked Alaskan king-crab legs
1/4 cup butter or margarine
1/4 teaspoon finely shredded lemon peel

1 teaspoon finely chopped tarragon or
  1/4 to 1/2 teaspoon dried leaf tarragon
1 tablespoon lemon juice

Thaw crab legs. Preheat broiler. Grease a broiling pan. Melt butter or margarine in a small saucepan. Stir in lemon peel, tarragon and lemon juice. Place crab legs on greased rack. Brush with butter sauce. Broil 3 to 5 inches from heat, 3 to 4 minutes. Baste once with butter sauce. Serve remaining butter sauce separately for dipping. Makes 2 servings.

Soups & Stews

Seafood soups and stews are often the same, although stew usually means heartier fare. Stews contain fish or shellfish, vegetables and seasonings simmered in a liquid. Hearty soups and stews can be turned into a feast when accompanied by a green salad and crusty bread to soak up the broth.

Shellfish and firm-texture fish, such as haddock, halibut, cod, sea bass and rockfish, contribute the best texture and flavor to soups and stews. High-fat, delicate, or soft-texture fish, such as sablefish, will fall apart when cooked in liquid. Strong-flavor fish, such as herring, anchovies and sardines, overpower other ingredients. A soup or stew may contain one type of fish, but will be more flavorful and interesting if several types are combined. Add chunks of fish to the pot last, then cook until they become firm and opaque.

Fish Stock is the base of many seafood soups and stews. It is quick to prepare, taking only 30 minutes for the bones to render their flavor. The liquid may be water or a combination of water and wine, to which vegetables, seasonings and any part of the fish—except the gills and viscera—are added. Crab, lobster and shrimp shells add a rich flavor to stock. Strain stock before it is used. Make stock in quantity by doubling or tripling the recipe. Freeze in amounts needed for individual recipes.

To make sauces, strain and boil the stock to reduce it and intensify flavor. A reduced stock is called *fumet,* but the terms stock and fumet are often used interchangeably. Because stock is often reduced, don't add salt until you're ready to use it.

Seafood soups and stews are an important part of the culinary heritage of coastal countries. French Bouillabaisse originated long ago in Marseilles as a humble dish—the fisherman's salvage of the day's catch. Today, Bouillabaisse has evolved into a glorious feast with many variations. Spain prides itself on Spanish Fish

Stew—spicy and tomato-based—rich with olive oil, garlic and saffron. And California's version of fish stew is Cioppino, a dish developed by immigrant fishermen of Italian and Portuguese descent.

Chowder comes from French *chaudiere,* a large kettle in which communal fish stews were made. Each fisherman contributed part of the day's catch to the pot. In the United States and Canada, chowder is synonymous with *clam chowder.* Reference to clam chowder is found in recipe books published before 1800. The first settlers made chowder with clams, salt pork, onions, milk and crackers—for thickening. Potatoes were added later. As chowder became popular farther south, tomatoes replaced milk. This version became known as Manhattan Clam Chowder—an absolute heresy to New Englanders.

Bisque is a creamy, rich puree of shellfish. This elegant and stylish preparation is often reserved for holidays or special occasions. To some Americans, Oyster Bisque is as traditional at Thanksgiving as turkey, and involves the same kind of ritualistic preparation.

Sea-Scallop Soup

Serve this lovely, delicate soup as a first course.

1/2 lb. sea scallops	1/4 cup dry sherry or white port
1/2 small carrot, peeled	Salt
1 green onion	White pepper
6 cups chicken broth	1 lime, thinly sliced
3 or 4 thin gingerroot slices	

Partially freeze scallops. Cut scallops into fine julienne pieces; set aside. Keeping carrot and green onion separate, cut into fine julienne shreds similar to thin noodles; set aside. In a medium saucepan, bring broth, gingerroot and sherry or port to a simmer. Cover and simmer 5 minutes. Remove and discard gingerroot slices. Add carrot shreds to broth; cook about 30 seconds. Add scallops; cook about 30 seconds longer. Remove pan from heat. Stir in green-onion shreds; season with salt and white pepper to taste. Pour into a tureen or serve in individual bowls. Garnish with lime slices. Makes 6 to 8 servings.

Soused Crab Soup

Scotch whiskey is the secret ingredient in this delicious crab soup.

3/4 lb. crabmeat	1 tablespoon all-purpose flour
1/4 cup butter or margarine	1 qt. milk (4 cups)
1 cup whipping cream	1/4 teaspoon salt
1/4 cup Scotch whiskey	1/8 teaspoon white pepper
1 tablespoon butter	Finely chopped parsley

Flake crabmeat; remove cartilage. Set aside. Melt 1/4 cup butter or margarine in a medium saucepan. Stir in flaked crabmeat, cream and whiskey. Over medium heat, stir until heated through; *do not boil.* Remove from heat; set aside. In a large saucepan, melt 1 tablespoon butter; stir in flour. Cook 1 to 2 minutes, stirring constantly. Gradually stir in 1 cup milk. Cook until slightly thickened, stirring constantly. Stir in remaining milk, crab mixture, salt and white pepper. Cook until very hot; *do not boil.* Pour into a tureen or serve in individual bowls. Garnish with parsley. Makes 4 to 6 servings.

Sea-Scallop Soup

Cioppino

Serve with lots of crusty French bread.

1-1/2 to 2 oz. dried Italian mushrooms
Water
1/4 cup olive oil
1 large onion, chopped
4 garlic cloves, minced
1 green bell pepper, chopped
4 large tomatoes, peeled, seeded, chopped
1/3 cup tomato puree
2 tablespoons tomato paste
2 cups Fish Stock, opposite
2 cups dry white wine
2 tablespoons finely chopped parsley

2 tablespoons finely chopped basil or
   1-1/2 teaspoons dried leaf basil
Pinch of sugar
Salt and black pepper
2 to 2-1/2 lbs. Dungeness crab,
   cleaned, cracked
18 small or medium hard-shell clams,
   scrubbed
1 lb. firm-texture skinless fish fillets,
   cut in 1-1/2- to 2-inch pieces
1 lb. medium shrimp,
   peeled, deveined

Thoroughly rinse mushrooms. In a small bowl, cover rinsed mushrooms with warm water; soak 20 minutes or until soft and pliable. Strain soaking liquid through several layers of cheesecloth; set aside. Coarsely chop soaked mushrooms; set aside. Heat oil in a large kettle. Add onion; sauté until soft and transparent. Add chopped mushrooms, garlic and green pepper. Cook 5 minutes longer. Add tomatoes, tomato puree, tomato paste, stock, wine, parsley and basil. Add 3 to 4 tablespoons reserved strained mushroom liquid. Add sugar, salt and black pepper to taste. Cover and simmer 20 minutes. Broth can be made ahead to this point and refrigerated 6 to 8 hours. At serving time, bring broth to a simmer. Add crab pieces; cover and cook 3 to 5 minutes. Add clams and fish pieces; cover and simmer 5 minutes longer. Add shrimp. Cook until shrimp become firm and turn pink, and clams open, 3 to 5 minutes. Discard clams that do not open. Serve from kettle or spoon into a tureen. Makes 6 to 8 servings.

Curry-Crab Soup

The compatible flavors of curry and crab blend especially well in this creamy soup.

3/4 lb. crabmeat
1/4 cup butter or margarine
1-1/2 tablespoons all-purpose flour
1 cup milk
1 qt. half and half (4 cups)
1/2 teaspoon or more curry powder

2 to 3 tablespoons dry sherry
Salt
White pepper
Pinch of red (cayenne) pepper
Finely chopped parsley or chives

Flake crabmeat; remove cartilage. Set aside. Melt butter or margarine in a large saucepan. Stir in flour. Stirring constantly, cook until smooth and bubbly. Slowly stir in milk. Continue stirring until mixture thickens slightly. Stir in half and half, flaked crabmeat, curry powder and sherry. Season with salt, white pepper and red pepper to taste. Stirring constantly, cook until very hot; *do not boil.* Pour into a tureen or serve in individual bowls. Garnish with parsley or chives. Makes 4 to 6 servings.

Cream of Shrimp & Dill Soup

Boiling the shrimp shells adds a rich flavor to this soup.

1-1/4 lbs. medium shrimp
3 (8-oz.) bottles clam juice
2 cups water
4 parsley sprigs
3/4 teaspoon finely chopped thyme or
   1/4 teaspoon dried leaf thyme
1/2 teaspoon finely chopped sage or
   1/4 teaspoon dried leaf sage
1/4 cup butter or margarine
1 medium onion, finely chopped
1 medium carrot, finely chopped

1 celery stalk, finely chopped
2 small leeks or 4 large green onions,
   white portions only, chopped
3 tablespoons all-purpose flour
1/2 cup whipping cream
1 tablespoon finely chopped dill or
   1/2 to 3/4 teaspoon dill weed
3 to 4 teaspoons lemon juice
Salt
White pepper

Shell and devein shrimp, reserving shells. Dice shelled shrimp; refrigerate until ready to use. In a large saucepan, combine shrimp shells, clam juice, water, parsley, thyme and sage. Bring to a boil; reduce heat. Cover and simmer 30 minutes. Strain liquid through a fine colander or strainer lined with several layers of cheesecloth; set aside. Wash saucepan. Over low heat, melt butter or margarine in clean saucepan. Add onion, carrot, celery and leeks or green onions. Cover and cook 15 minutes or until tender. Stir in flour; cook 3 to 4 minutes, stirring constantly. Stir in reserved liquid and all but 1/4 cup diced shrimp. Bring to a boil; reduce heat and simmer 5 minutes, stirring occasionally. Pour into a blender or food processor fitted with a metal blade; process until smooth. Return to saucepan. Add cream, dill, lemon juice and reserved diced shrimp. Gently simmer 5 minutes. Season with salt and white pepper to taste. Serve warm or cold. Spoon into a tureen or serve in individual bowls. Makes 6 servings.

Fish Stock

Save trimmings from fish and freeze them for stock.

2 to 3 lbs. fish bones, heads and tails
6 cups water
2 cups dry white wine
1 onion, thinly sliced
1 leek or 1 onion, thinly sliced

1 carrot, thinly sliced
6 parsley sprigs
1 bay leaf
4 black peppercorns

Rinse fish parts; remove gills, if necessary. Crack large bones. Place trimmings and bones in a large kettle. Add water and wine. Bring to a boil. Boil gently 5 minutes, skimming foam from surface until surface is clear. Reduce to a simmer. Add onion, leek or additional onion, carrot, parsley and bay leaf. Simmer 20 minutes, skimming foam from surface until surface is clear. Add peppercorns. Simmer 10 minutes longer. Strain stock through a fine colander or sieve lined with several layers of cheesecloth. Discard bones and vegetables. Season stock when used in a soup, stew or sauce. Makes about 7 cups.

Spanish Fish Stew

This hearty fish stew was inspired by a trip to the Mediterranean.

3 tablespoons olive oil or vegetable oil
1 large onion, chopped
3 garlic cloves, minced
1/2 cup diced green bell pepper
1 (16-oz.) can whole peeled tomatoes,
    undrained, chopped
2 (8-oz.) bottles clam juice
2-3/4 cups water
2 tablespoons tomato paste
1 bay leaf
1/2 teaspoon ground turmeric

1 teaspoon finely chopped thyme or
    1/2 teaspoon dried leaf thyme
1/4 teaspoon or more crushed fennel seeds
Pinch of sugar
1/8 to 1/4 teaspoon saffron powder,
    if desired
Salt
Freshly ground black pepper
1-1/2 lbs. skinless firm-texture fish fillets
12 to 18 peeled, deveined medium shrimp

Heat oil in a large kettle over medium heat. Add onion, garlic and green pepper; sauté until onion is soft and transparent. Add tomatoes and liquid, clam juice, water, tomato paste, bay leaf, turmeric, thyme, fennel seeds, sugar and saffron, if desired. Cover and simmer 15 minutes. Add salt and black pepper to taste. Cut fish into 1-inch pieces. Add fish pieces and shrimp to soup. Simmer gently 4 to 5 minutes or until fish becomes firm and turns opaque, and shrimp becomes firm and turns pink. Remove and discard bay leaf. Spoon stew into a tureen or serve in individual bowls. Makes 6 servings.

Oyster Stew

Jars of fresh-shucked oysters are available in most fish markets.

3 tablespoons butter or margarine
3 large shallots or
    1 small onion, finely chopped
1 cup diced celery
1 bay leaf
Finely shredded peel of 1 large lemon
1-1/2 qts. half and half (6 cups)

3/4 teaspoon salt
1/2 teaspoon paprika
1/8 teaspoon red (cayenne) pepper
1-1/2 to 2 teaspoons Worcestershire sauce
24 to 36 shucked oysters with liquor
2 tablespoons butter or margarine
Paprika

Melt 3 tablespoons butter or margarine in a large kettle. Add shallots or onion and celery. Over medium heat, sauté until soft. Add bay leaf and lemon peel; sauté 1 minute longer. Add half and half, salt, paprika, red pepper and Worcestershire sauce. Heat until very hot; *do not boil.* If oysters are large, cut in half. Add oysters and liquor to kettle. Cook about 3 minutes, stirring constantly, until edges of oysters start to curl and become firm. Do not overcook. Taste and adjust seasonings. Divide oysters among 6 serving bowls. Ladle in broth. Cut 2 tablespoons butter or margarine into 6 pats; float 1 pat in each bowl. Garnish with paprika. Makes 6 servings.

Bouillabaisse, page 104

Bouillabaisse

Bouillabaisse is traditionally made with 5 or 6 kinds of fish and shellfish.

Soup Croutons, opposite
Rouille, see below
1/4 cup olive oil
2 medium onions, chopped
2 medium leeks, white and
    pale green portions only, chopped
4 garlic cloves, minced
4 cups Fish Stock, page 101
1 cup dry white wine
4 medium tomatoes, peeled, chopped
1/2 teaspoon fennel seeds, crushed
1/4 cup chopped parsley

1-1/2 teaspoons finely chopped thyme or
    1/2 to 3/4 teaspoon dried leaf thyme
1 bay leaf
1 teaspoon saffron threads or
    1/8 teaspoon powdered saffron
Salt
Freshly ground pepper
2 lbs. firm-texture, skinless fish fillets
1 to 1-1/2 lbs. cooked,
    in-shell lobster tails, thawed if frozen
18 mussels, debearded
18 scallops

Rouille:
1 large, red bell pepper or
    2 (2-oz.) jars sliced pimientos,
    drained
1/2 cup soft white breadcrumbs
1/4 cup milk or water

1/4 to 1/2 teaspoon hot-pepper flakes
2 or 3 garlic cloves
1/4 cup olive oil
1 to 3 tablespoons broth from Bouillabaisse
Salt

Prepare Soup Croutons; set aside. Begin Rouille preparation. Heat oil in a large heavy kettle. Add onions, leeks and garlic; over medium heat, sauté about 5 minutes. Add stock, wine, tomatoes, fennel seeds, parsley, thyme, bay leaf and saffron. Bring to a boil; reduce heat and simmer 10 minutes. Season with salt and pepper to taste. Cut fish into pieces, about 2" x 1-1/2". Add fish pieces to stock mixture; gently simmer 2 to 3 minutes. With a heavy knife or kitchen shears, cut lobster tails into 1-1/2-inch pieces, cutting through flesh and shell. Scrub mussels with a brush to remove dirt from shells; discard any mussels that do not close. Add lobster pieces and cleaned mussels to stock mixture. Cook until mussels open, 3 to 6 minutes; discard any mussels that do not open. During final 2 minutes of cooking, add scallops. Finish preparing Rouille. Remove and discard bay leaf. Serve soup from kettle or spoon into a tureen. Place 1 or 2 croutons in individual bowls; ladle broth over croutons. Arrange fish and shellfish on top. Serve Rouille and remaining croutons separately. Makes 8 servings. -

Rouille:
Roast bell pepper over an open flame or in broiler until skin is charred and blistered. Place in a large plastic food-storage bag; set aside 5 to 10 minutes to steam. Peel blistered pepper; cut in half. Remove and discard seeds. In a medium bowl, combine breadcrumbs and milk or water; let stand 5 minutes. Squeeze crumbs dry; discard liquid. In a blender or food processor fitted with a metal blade, process bell-pepper strips or pimientos, hot-pepper flakes, garlic and soaked breadcrumbs until smooth. Gradually add oil until thoroughly blended. At serving time, stir in broth. Add salt to taste. Spoon into a small serving bowl. Serve separately. Rouille can be spooned onto croutons to float in soup or spooned directly into Bouillabaisse. Makes about 3/4 cup.

How to Make Rouille for Bouillabaise

1/To make Rouille, combine breadcrumbs and milk. Let stand about 5 minutes; squeeze out and discard milk.

2/Add oil to pureed mixture, a little at a time, until thoroughly blended. Add broth at serving time.

Soup Croutons

Serve these crisp slices with any soup or stew.

**30 slices bagette French bread,
  1/4 inch thick**

**1/4 cup olive oil
2 to 3 garlic cloves**

Preheat oven to 350F (175C). Brush bread slices lightly with oil. Place on baking sheets. Toast in oven until dry and golden brown. Cool on racks. Rub croutons with garlic cloves. Makes 30 croutons.

The best buy is whole fish you cut up yourself. It is less expensive and you have the bones and trimmings for stock.

Manhattan Clam Chowder

The great flavor of this Manhattan clam chowder comes from the tomato base.

6 lbs. quahog clams, chowder clams or
   cherrystone clams
3 cups water
6 bacon slices
1 large onion, chopped
3/4 cup finely diced carrot
3/4 cup finely diced celery
1/2 cup finely diced green bell pepper
2 garlic cloves, minced
2 thyme sprigs or
   1/2 teaspoon dried leaf thyme

1 bay leaf
About 3 cups bottled clam juice,
   fish stock or water
1 to 2 tablespoons tomato paste
1 (16-oz.) can whole peeled tomatoes,
   undrained, coarsely chopped
3 medium potatoes, peeled,
   cut in 1/2- to 3/4-inch pieces
Salt and black pepper
Finely chopped parsley

Scrub clams with a brush to remove sand from shells; discard clams that do not close. Place in a large kettle with water. Cover and cook until clams open, 7 to 10 minutes. Discard any clams that do not open. Use a slotted spoon to place cooked clams in a large bowl. Holding over kettle to catch juices, remove clam meat from open shells; discard shells. Coarsely chop clams; set aside. Strain liquid through several layers of cheesecloth; set aside. Rinse and dry kettle. In same kettle, cook bacon until crisp. Drain on paper towels; crumble cooked bacon. Reserve 1 to 2 tablespoons bacon fat in kettle over medium heat. Add onion, carrot, celery, green pepper and garlic; sauté until onion is soft and transparent. Add thyme and bay leaf. Measure clam liquid; add bottled clam juice, fish stock or water to make 6 cups. Add to onion mixture. Stir in tomato paste and tomatoes with juice. Add chopped clams and potatoes. Cover kettle; gently simmer 1 hour. Season with salt and black pepper. Ladle chowder into a tureen or serve in individual bowls. Garnish with crumbled bacon and parsley. Makes 8 (1-1/2-cup) servings.

Variation

Conch Chowder: Substitute 1-1/2 cups ground conch for clams. Substitute 6 cups Fish Stock, page 101, for clam liquid.

Conch, pronounced konk, *encased in a handsome spiral shell, inhabits temperate or warm waters. The muscle is edible, but is tough and must be tenderized. This is done by pounding or grinding.*

Fisherman's Chowder

Use several types of fish, such as cod, pollock, drum, porgy or angler, for best flavor and interest.

3 oz. salt pork, diced
1 medium onion, chopped
3/4 cup diced celery
1 garlic clove, minced
1 bay leaf
3/4 teaspoon finely chopped thyme or
　1/4 teaspoon dried leaf thyme
1/2 teaspoon chopped sage or
　1/8 to 1/4 teaspoon dried leaf sage
2 tablespoons all-purpose flour
3 medium potatoes, peeled,
　cut in 3/4-inch cubes

4 cups Fish Stock, page 101, or
　2 (8-oz.) bottles clam juice
　plus 2 cups water
1-1/2 lbs. firm-texture skinless fish fillets
1 pint half and half (2 cups)
Salt
Freshly ground black pepper
Pinch red (cayenne) pepper
Chopped parsley
About 2 cups toasted croutons or
　oyster crackers

Sauté salt pork in a large kettle until most of fat is rendered out and pork begins to brown. Add onion; sauté until soft and transparent. Add celery, garlic, bay leaf, thyme and sage. Stirring frequently, cook 2 to 3 minutes. Stir in flour. Stirring constantly, cook 1 to 2 minutes longer. Stir in potatoes and stock or clam juice and water. Cover and simmer until potatoes are tender, 20 to 25 minutes. Cut fillets into 1-inch pieces; add to stock mixture. Simmer 5 minutes or until fish turns opaque and becomes firm. Remove and discard bay leaf. Stir in half and half; heat through. Add salt, black pepper and red pepper to taste. Spoon into a tureen or serve in individual bowls. Garnish with parsley. Serve croutons or oyster crackers separately. Makes 6 servings.

New England Clam Chowder

This simple but delicious traditional favorite uses canned clams.

3 or 4 bacon slices, diced
1 onion, finely chopped
1/2 cup finely diced celery
2 tablespoons all-purpose flour
2 (6-1/2-oz.) cans chopped or
　minced clams, undrained
2 (8-oz.) bottles clam juice

3 medium potatoes, peeled,
　cut in 1/2-inch cubes
1 bay leaf
2-1/2 cups half and half
Salt and pepper
Paprika
Finely chopped parsley

In a large kettle, fry bacon until crisp; drain on paper towels. Reserve 1 to 2 tablespoons bacon fat in kettle. Add onion and celery; sauté until onion is soft and transparent. Stir in flour; cook 1 minute. Drain juice from clams into kettle; reserve clams. Stir in bottled clam juice. Add cooked bacon, potatoes and bay leaf. Cover and simmer 20 minutes or until potatoes are tender. Add half and half and reserved clams. Add salt and pepper to taste. Cook until heated through. Remove and discard bay leaf. Serve from kettle or spoon into a tureen. Garnish with paprika and parsley. Makes 4 to 6 servings.

Billibi

This elegant mussel soup is an adaptation of a soup first served at Maxim's in Paris.

2 lbs. mussels
1/2 lb. mushrooms, chopped
1/2 cup chopped shallots
1-1/4 cups dry white wine
3/4 cup water
4 parsley sprigs

1/2 teaspoon dried leaf thyme
2 egg yolks
1-1/2 cups whipping cream
Salt and pepper
Finely chopped parsley or watercress sprigs

Scrub mussels with a brush to remove dirt from shells; pull off beards. Discard any mussels that do not close. Place cleaned mussels in a kettle with mushrooms, shallots, wine, water, parsley sprigs and thyme. Bring to a simmer. Cover and cook 3 to 5 minutes or until mussels open; after 2 minutes, turn mussels with a large spoon. Using a slotted spoon, place cooked mussels in a bowl. Discard any mussels that do not open. Let cooking liquid stand and settle 3 to 5 minutes. Remove cooked mussels from shells; pull off black rims. Discard shells; set mussels aside. Strain cooking liquid through 4 or 5 layers of cheesecloth into a medium saucepan. Press down vegetables with back of a spoon to extract as much liquid as possible; discard vegetables. Bring liquid to a simmer. In a small bowl, beat together egg yolks and cream. Stir 1/4 cup hot liquid into egg-yolk mixture, then blend into remaining liquid. Stirring constantly, heat until soup thickens slightly. Season with salt and pepper to taste. Place reserved mussels in a tureen or in individual bowls. Ladle soup over mussels. Garnish with parsley or watercress. Makes 6 to 8 servings.

Smoked-Haddie Chowder

Finnan haddie adds a subtle smoked favor to the chowder.

1/4 lb. salt pork, rind removed
Water
1 large onion, chopped
1/2 cup diced celery
2 medium carrots, sliced
3 medium potatoes, unpeeled,
  cut in 1/2-inch cubes

1 bay leaf
3-1/2 cups milk
1-1/2 lbs. finnan haddie,
  cut in 3/4-inch chunks
1/2 cup whipping cream
Salt and pepper

In a medium saucepan, blanch salt pork 5 minutes in boiling water to cover. Drain; cut blanched salt pork into 1/4-inch cubes. In a large kettle, brown salt-pork cubes over medium-high heat, stirring frequently. Add onion, celery and carrots. Sauté until onion is soft and transparent. Add potatoes, 1-3/4 cups water, bay leaf and milk. Cover and simmer 10 to 15 minutes. Add finnan haddie; simmer 10 minutes longer. Remove and discard bay leaf. Stir in cream. Add salt and pepper to taste. Serve from kettle or spoon into a tureen. Makes 8 servings.

How to Make Billibi

1/Remove beards from mussels. Press together or tap shells with your fingers; discard mussels that stay open.

2/Remove cooked mussels from shells; pull off black rims. Discard mussels that do not open during cooking.

Oyster Bisque

A velvety smooth soup to delight oyster lovers.

1/2 cup uncooked long-grain white rice
3 cups Fish Stock, page 101,
   or chicken broth
2 tablespoons butter or margarine
1 pint shucked oysters or
   2 (8- or 10-oz.) jars shucked oysters
   with liquor

1-1/4 cups whipping cream
Salt
White pepper
2 tablespoons dry sherry
1 teaspoon lemon juice
Finely chopped parsley or watercress sprigs
Slivered lemon peel

In a large saucepan, combine rice, 2 cups Fish Stock or chicken broth and butter or margarine. Bring to a boil; reduce heat so mixture simmers gently. Cover and simmer until rice is *very* soft, 25 to 30 minutes. In a blender or food processor fitted with a metal blade, process cooked rice mixture and oysters with liquor until completely smooth. Return mixture to saucepan; add remaining 1 cup stock or broth and cream. Add salt and white pepper to taste. Stir in sherry and lemon juice. Heat bisque until hot, stirring frequently; *do not boil.* Taste for seasoning, adding more sherry, lemon juice, salt and white pepper, if desired. Pour into a tureen or serve in individual bowls. Garnish with parsley or watercress and lemon peel. Makes 6 to 8 servings.

Appetizers & Salads

Appetizers are bite-size morsels of food, and as the name suggests, are designed to stimulate appetites. Seafood makes especially good appetizers because it's light and leaves room so you can enjoy the meal ahead. Seafood appetizers make excellent party fare.

Guests will enjoy Bagna Cauda—literally translated *hot bath.* Serve this garlicky dip warm with raw-vegetable pieces and thinly sliced French bread. Or, for something slightly exotic, treat your guests to Taramasalata, dramatically presented in a hollowed-out eggplant and served with toasted pita bread.

Prawns Pacifica, Sardines in Dill Sauce and most of the dips and spreads featured in this chapter are do-ahead party foods. Terrine de Coquilles and Salmon Mousseline with Tomato-Dill Butter make elegant first courses for a dinner party. Simplest of all are the quintessential oysters on-the-half-shell. Although no recipe is given, freshly shucked oysters are presented simply—on-the-half-shell—with a squeeze of lemon and a few grinds of pepper or with Shallot Sauce, page 153. Transformed into a hot appetizer, these mollusks become Oysters Rockefeller. My recipe is a modern, lighter version of the classic dish. Another updated classic is Coquilles Saint Jacques Nouvelle. Scallops are simmered in wine, then served on a layer of spinach, mushrooms and onions.

If you plan a casual get together, serve appetizers that have universal appeal. Then your less-adventurous guests will enjoy themselves. If you offer several appetizers, make one of them special and different. Pickled Herring, Tapenade, Mussels Vinaigrette, Seviche and Brandade Provençal are all out of the ordinary.

Some of my seafood salads, such as Shrimp Salad with Dijon Cream, are perfect as a first course. Others, like California Tuna Salad, can be served as the main course of a luncheon or light supper.

I have included several old favorites, including Niçoise Salad. My version, Layered Niçoise Salad, uses traditional colorful ingredients, but layers them in a large bowl. It is perfect for buffet service. Pasta salads are always favorites. Seafood-Pasta Salad served with Pesto Vinaigrette is no exception. Another new favorite is Calamari Salad, featuring rings of cooked squid tossed in an assertive vinaigrette dressing.

Classic Crab Louis

The origin of Crab Louis is disputable, but this version is indisputably delicious.

Louis Dressing, see below
1 head iceberg lettuce
3/4 to 1 lb. crabmeat
2 medium tomatoes, cut in wedges

2 hard-cooked eggs, cut in wedges
Capers
Ripe olives

Louis Dressing:
1/2 cup Mayonnaise, page 144,
  or other mayonnaise
1/2 cup dairy sour cream
3 to 4 tablespoons tomato-based chili sauce

1 tablespoon lemon juice
Few drops hot-pepper sauce
1/4 cup diced green bell pepper
1/4 cup sliced green onions

Prepare Louis Dressing. Cover; refrigerate at least 1 hour to let flavors blend. Rinse, core and drain lettuce. Pull off 4 large outer leaves; place 1 lettuce leaf on each of 4 plates. Shred enough remaining lettuce to make 6 cups. Refrigerate any remaining lettuce for another use. Place shredded lettuce on lettuce leaves. Flake crabmeat; remove any cartilage. Arrange crabmeat evenly over shredded lettuce. Spoon about half of dressing over crabmeat. Garnish each plate with tomato wedges, egg wedges, capers and olives. Serve remaining dressing separately. Makes 4 servings.

Louis Dressing:
Combine ingredients in a small bowl; blend well. Makes about 1-1/3 cups.

Variation
Shrimp Louis: Substitute cooked, shelled tiny shrimp for crabmeat.

Heavily salted cooking water draws sea salt from shellfish, resulting in a more pleasing flavor.

Layered Niçoise Salad

This French classic makes a beautiful buffet dish when layered in a glass serving bowl.

Vinaigrette Dijonnaise, see below
2 (6-1/2-oz.) cans water-pack,
 solid-pack albacore tuna, drained
3/4 lb. new or red potatoes, cooked, peeled
1 head romaine lettuce
Freshly ground pepper
1 small cucumber, thinly sliced

1 (2-oz.) can flat anchovies, rinsed, drained
10 to 12 small niçoise olives or
 12 small to medium pitted, whole,
 ripe olives, cut in half crosswise
2 hard-cooked eggs, cut in wedges
1 tomato, cut in wedges

Vinaigrette Dijonnaise:
4 to 6 tablespoons white-wine vinegar
1-1/2 tablespoons Dijon-style mustard
1 teaspoon minced garlic
1/4 teaspoon sugar

1/2 teaspoon salt
Freshly ground pepper
1 cup olive oil

Prepare Vinaigrette Dijonnaise; set aside. Flake tuna into a small bowl. Toss with 1/3 cup Vinaigrette Dijonnaise. Cover; refrigerate at least 2 hours. Thinly slice potatoes; place in a shallow dish. Pour 1/2 cup Vinaigrette Dijonnaise over potatoes. Cover; refrigerate at least 2 hours. Remove outer leaves from lettuce. Line a shallow serving bowl with lettuce leaves. Tear enough remaining leaves to make 5 to 6 cups. Refrigerate any remaining lettuce for another use. Toss torn lettuce with remaining Vinaigrette Dijonnaise. Spoon into lettuce-lined bowl. Lift potatoes from dressing; layer over lettuce. Cover with several grinds of pepper. Drain excess dressing from tuna; discard. Top potatoes with a layer of marinated tuna. Overlap cucumber slices to cover tuna. Arrange anchovies like spokes of a wheel over cucumbers. Place olives in center. Arrange egg wedges and tomato wedges around edge of salad. Makes 6 servings.

Vinaigrette Dijonnaise:
In a medium bowl, blend vinegar, mustard, garlic, sugar and salt. Add pepper to taste. Using a whisk, slowly beat in oil. Dressing will be tart. Makes 1-1/4 cups.

Brandade Provençal

In France, brandade is spread on bits of toast, then sprinkled with cheese and broiled.

1 lb. salt cod
Water
1 or 2 garlic cloves

About 1/3 cup whipping cream
About 1/3 cup olive oil
Finely chopped parsley

Place cod in a large bowl; cover with cold water. Refrigerate at least 12 hours, changing water twice. Rinse soaked cod; place in a large saucepan. Cover with cold water; bring to a boil. Reduce heat; simmer 7 to 10 minutes or until fish tests done. Drain and flake fish, discarding bones. In a blender or food processor fitted with a metal blade, process flaked fish and garlic until evenly chopped. With machine running, gradually pour in 1/3 cup cream and 1/3 cup oil. Process until smooth and spreadable. Add more cream and oil, if needed. Spoon into a serving dish; sprinkle with parsley. Makes about 2 cups.

Calamari Salad

A colorful and affordable salad using squid.

3 lbs. squid, cleaned
1 cup diced red or green bell pepper
1/2 medium, red onion, thinly sliced,
  separated into rings
1/2 cup sliced ripe olives
2 tablespoons finely chopped parsley
1 tablespoon drained capers, rinsed
1/4 cup red-wine vinegar
1/4 teaspoon sugar
2 garlic cloves, minced

2 teaspoons finely chopped oregano or
  3/4 teaspoon dried leaf oregano
1 tablespoon finely chopped basil or
  1 teaspoon dried leaf basil
3/4 cup olive oil or vegetable oil
Salt
Freshly ground black pepper
Lettuce or other salad greens
Cherry tomatoes or tomato wedges

Cut squid bodies crosswise into 1/4- to 1/2-inch slices. Cut tentacles crosswise in halves or quarters. Bring a kettle of salted water to a boil. Add squid pieces; simmer 15 to 30 seconds or until squid turns opaque. Remove with a slotted spoon; rinse with cold water. Drain again; pat dry with paper towels. In a large bowl, toss together cooked squid, bell pepper, onion rings, olives, parsley and capers. In a small bowl, combine vinegar, sugar, garlic, oregano and basil. Using a whisk, beat in oil a little at a time. Pour dressing over salad; toss to distribute. Season with salt and black pepper to taste. Line a platter or individual plates with lettuce or other salad greens. Mound salad on greens. Garnish with tomatoes. Makes 4 or 5 main-dish or 6 to 8 appetizer servings.

Italian White-Bean & Tuna Salad

Soaking raw onions in ice water eliminates any harsh flavor and sweetens them.

1 cup dry small white beans
Water
1 cup chopped red onion
1 (6-1/2-oz.) can oil-pack,
  solid-pack albacore tuna
1/3 cup olive oil

2 teaspoons each balsamic vinegar and
  red-wine vinegar, or
  1 tablespoon red-wine vinegar
1/2 teaspoon salt
Freshly ground pepper
Finely chopped parsley

Sort and rinse beans; place in a medium saucepan. Add cold water to cover. Over medium-high heat, bring to a boil, uncovered; boil 2 minutes. Remove from heat; cover and let beans soak 1 hour. Discard soaking water; rinse beans under cold running water. In same saucepan, cover beans with fresh water; bring to a boil. Reduce heat; simmer 50 to 60 minutes or until beans are tender. Drain; rinse under cold water. Drain thoroughly. Meanwhile, soak onion in ice water 15 minutes. Drain; pat dry with paper towels. In a medium bowl, toss together cooked and drained beans, soaked onion, tuna with oil, olive oil and vinegar. Season with salt, pepper and more vinegar, if desired. Garnish with parsley. Serve at room temperature or slightly chilled. Makes 6 servings.

Tip: Balsamic vinegar contains balsam. It is available in many supermarkets and specialty-food stores.

How to Clean Squid for Calamari Salad

 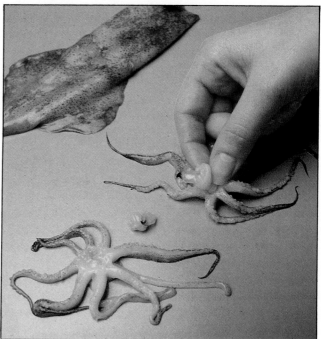

1/Pull gently to separate tentacles, viscera and ink sac from body. Pull out transparent sword-shape pen from body.

2/Cut off tentacles above eyes. Reserve tentacles. Squeeze the hard, round beak from base of tentacles. Discard beak.

Green Goddess Seafood Salad

The classic dressing was created by San Francisco Palace Hotel chefs in the 1920s.

1-1/4 cups Mayonnaise, page 144,
  or other mayonnaise
1 (2-oz.) can flat anchovies, drained,
  finely chopped
2 tablespoons tarragon vinegar or
  white-wine vinegar
2 tablespoons finely chopped parsley
2 tablespoons finely chopped chives or
  green-onion tops
1 small garlic clove, minced

3/4 teaspoon finely chopped tarragon or
  1/4 teaspoon dried leaf tarragon
About 3 qts. torn romaine lettuce or
  combination or romaine and
  iceberg lettuce
3/4 to 1 lb. cooked, shelled medium shrimp,
  langostinos, crabmeat or lobster
1 avocado, sliced
12 to 18 cherry tomatoes or tomato wedges
12 to 18 ripe olives

In a small bowl, combine mayonnaise, anchovies, vinegar, parsley, chives or green-onion tops, garlic and tarragon. Cover and refrigerate several hours to let flavors blend. In a large bowl, toss about half the mayonnaise mixture with lettuce. Divide lettuce mixture among 6 plates. Spoon shrimp, langostinos, crabmeat or lobster evenly over lettuce mixture. Garnish each with avocado, tomatoes and olives. Serve remaining dressing separately. Makes 6 servings.

Seafood-Pasta Salad

Accented by a pesto dressing, this salad features a variety of shellfish.

Pesto Vinaigrette, see below
1 (12-oz.) pkg. spiral pasta
Water
Salt
1 lb. squid, cleaned
1 lb. small to medium shrimp,
   peeled, deveined
1 lb. scallops

1 cup fresh or frozen tiny green peas
1 small red bell pepper, diced,
   or 1 (2-oz.) jar sliced pimientos
1/2 small red onion, thinly sliced,
   separated into rings
1/4 cup freshly grated Parmesan
   cheese (3/4 oz.)
Salt and black pepper

Pesto Vinaigrette:
2/3 cup loosely packed basil leaves or
   1-1/2 tablespoons dried leaf basil
   and 2/3 cup parsley sprigs
2/3 cup olive oil
1/3 cup freshly grated Parmesan cheese
   (1 oz.)

2 to 3 tablespoons red-wine vinegar
2 garlic cloves, minced
3/4 teaspoon salt
1/2 teaspoon sugar

Prepare Pesto Vinaigrette; set aside. Cook pasta in boiling salted water following package directions; drain. Rinse with cold water; drain again. Cut squid bodies in 1/4-inch crosswise slices. Trim long tentacles; cut tentacles crosswise in halves or quarters. Bring a kettle of salted water to a boil. Add squid; bring water back to a simmer. Cook 3 minutes. Use a slotted spoon to remove squid; drain on paper towels. Bring water to a boil again; add shrimp. Cook 2 to 3 minutes or until shrimp become firm and turn pink. Use slotted spoon to remove shrimp; drain on paper towels. Add scallops to simmering water. Cook 1 to 2 minutes or until scallops become firm and opaque. Use slotted spoon to remove scallops; drain on paper towels. Seafood and pasta should be free of excess water. In a large bowl, combine cooked pasta, cooked seafood, uncooked peas, bell pepper or pimientos, onion and Parmesan cheese. Pour Pesto Vinaigrette over salad; toss to distribute. Taste and adjust seasonings, adding salt and black pepper to taste. Makes 6 to 8 servings.

Pesto Vinaigrette:
In a blender or food processor fitted with a metal blade, process all ingredients until smooth. Makes about 1-1/4 cups.

Variation
Substitute cooked lobster or langostino for squid.

Albacore, also called white *or* white-meat tuna, *is the finest tuna canned. Light or light-meat tuna comes from other varieties of tuna.*

Shrimp Salad with Dijon Cream

The delicate flavors of shrimp and asparagus are complemented by a mild dressing.

Water
Salt
3/4 to 1 lb. small to medium shrimp
1/2 cup Mayonnaise, page 144,
   or other mayonnaise
1-1/2 to 2 tablespoons Dijon-style mustard

2 teaspoons lemon juice
1/3 cup whipping cream
White pepper
24 slender asparagus spears
Romaine lettuce
1 lemon, scored, thinly sliced

Bring a kettle of lightly salted water to a boil. Add shrimp; cook 2 to 3 minutes or until shrimp become firm and turn pink. Drain; immediately plunge into cold water to stop cooking. Shell and devein shrimp. Refrigerate to chill. In a medium bowl, combine mayonnaise, mustard and lemon juice. In a small bowl, whip cream until soft peaks form; fold into mayonnaise mixture. Season with salt and white pepper to taste. Spoon into a medium serving bowl. Cover and refrigerete until serving time. Wash and trim asparagus, peeling stalks if desired. In a large skillet, bring 1 to 2 inches water to a boil. Add trimmed asparagus; cook until crisp-tender. Plunge into cold water to stop cooking. Drain; set aside or refrigerate. Arrange romaine leaves on a platter or on 4 to 6 salad plates. Arrange cooked asparagus spears over lettuce on platter, or place 4 to 6 asparagus spears on each plate. Arrange cooked shrimp over top. Garnish with lemon slices. Serve dressing separately. Makes 4 to 6 servings.

Variation

Substitute blanched broccoli, green beans or zucchini strips for asparagus spears.

California Tuna Salad

An appealing light salad that's perfect for warm summer days.

2 medium oranges
1/4 cup Mayonnaise, page 144,
   or other mayonnaise
1/4 cup plain yogurt
Salt
Pinch of red (cayenne) pepper
2 (6-1/2-oz.) cans oil- or water-pack,
   solid-pack albacore tuna, drained

1 cup thinly sliced celery
1/2 cup seedless grapes, cut in halves
Lettuce leaves
1/4 cup sliced almonds, lightly toasted
4 small seedless-grape clusters

Finely shred peel of 1 orange, making 2 teaspoons shredded peel. Peel remaining orange. Remove white membrane from both oranges. Slice peeled oranges crosswise; set aside. In a small bowl, combine shredded orange peel, mayonnaise and yogurt. Season with salt and red pepper to taste. In a medium bowl, break tuna into chunks. Add celery and grape halves; toss gently. Fold in mayonnaise mixture. Line individual serving plates or a large platter with lettuce leaves. Mound tuna salad in center. Scatter almonds over top. Arrange orange slices and grape clusters on side of each plate. Makes 4 main-dish servings.

Salmon Mousseline

Start your next dinner party with this elegant appetizer.

Tomato-Dill Butter, see below
1 lb. skinless salmon fillets or
   1-1/4 lbs. salmon steaks
2 egg whites
1-3/4 cups whipping cream
1 teaspoon salt
1/8 teaspoon white pepper

1 large bunch spinach, stems removed
1 tablespoon butter
1/4 cup water
Salt
White pepper
Dill sprigs or chopped chives

Tomato-Dill Butter:
1 tablespoon butter
1 medium shallot or 1 large green onion,
   white portion only, chopped
2 medium tomatoes, peeled, seeded, chopped
4 teaspoons finely chopped dill or
   1 teaspoon dill weed

1/4 cup butter, room temperature
Salt
White pepper

Prepare Tomato-Dill Butter; set aside. Preheat oven to 350F (175C). Butter 6 individual soufflé dishes, ramekins or timbale molds. If using salmon steaks, remove skin and bones. Cut salmon into pieces. In a blender or food processor fitted with a metal blade, puree salmon pieces. With machine running, add egg whites, cream, 1 teaspoon salt and 1/8 teaspoon white pepper. Process until blended. Spoon salmon mixture into a medium bowl. Cover and refrigerate until chilled. Spoon chilled salmon mixture into dishes or molds until half full. Center 1 tablespoon Tomato-Dill Butter on top of each. Fill molds to top with remaining salmon mixture, completely encasing butter. Tap molds gently on counter to remove air bubbles. Smooth tops with a spatula. Place molds in a large baking pan. Pour boiling water into baking pan to a depth of 1 to 2 inches or half depth of molds. Bake 20 to 30 minutes or until a skewer inserted in center comes out clean. Meanwhile, stack 10 to 12 spinach leaves on top of one another; roll lengthwise, jelly-roll fashion. Cut crosswise in 1/2-inch slices. Repeat with remaining leaves. Place butter and water in a large skillet; bring to a simmer. Add spinach; cook about 30 seconds or until tender. Drain off liquid; season spinach with salt and white pepper to taste. Spoon evenly onto individual serving plates. Run a sharp knife around edge of each hot mold. Invert mold in center of spinach; remove mold. Garnish tops of mousseline with dill sprigs or chives. Makes 6 servings.

Tomato-Dill Butter:
Melt 1 tablespoon butter in a medium saucepan. Add shallot or green onion; sauté until soft. Add tomatoes; stirring frequently, cook until most of liquid evaporates. Tomato mixture will be thicker than canned tomato sauce. *Do not overcook;* mixture scorches easily. Cool to room temperature. In a blender or food processor fitted with a metal blade, process tomato mixture and dill until smooth. Add 1/4 cup butter. Process until blended. Season with salt and white pepper to taste. Makes about 1/2 cup.

How to Make Salmon Mousseline

1/Fill molds half full with salmon mixture. Top with 1 tablespoon Tomato-Dill Butter. Cover completely with remaining salmon mixture.

2/Stack spinach leaves on top of one another; roll lengthwise, jelly-roll fashion. Cut crosswise in 1/4- to 1/2-inch slices.

Smoked Fish with Horseradish Cream

Fresh horseradish varies in intensity with the time of year it is harvested.

1 cup whipping cream
1-1/2 teaspoons sugar
2 to 4 tablespoons grated fresh horseradish
1 to 2 tablespoons white vinegar
Salt
White pepper
1 teaspoon chopped chives, dill or
   parsley or a combination

1 lb. smoked trout, sturgeon, salmon or
   other smoked fish, thinly sliced
Pumpernickel or other dark bread,
   thinly sliced
Unsalted butter

In a medium bowl, whip cream and sugar until soft peaks form. Fold in horseradish and vinegar. Add salt and white pepper to taste. Spoon into a small serving bowl. Sprinkle with chives, dill, parsley or combination. Arrange sliced fish and bread on a platter. Let guests butter bread and top with smoked fish. Serve horseradish cream as an accompaniment. Makes 8 to 10 servings.

Variation

To substitute prepared horseradish for fresh horseradish, omit sugar and vinegar from recipe. Whip cream as above; add 1 to 2 tablespoons prepared horseradish. For a stronger flavor, use more horseradish.

Oysters Rockefeller

A layer of rock salt not only keeps shells from tipping but keeps the oysters hot.

24 oysters on-the-half-shell
Rock salt
1/2 cup butter or margarine
4 medium shallots, chopped
1/4 cup chopped fennel sprigs or
   1/4 to 1/2 teaspoon dried
   leaf tarragon

1/4 cup chopped parsley
2 cups watercress or torn spinach leaves
2 to 4 tablespoons Pernod or
   other anise-flavored liqueur
Salt
Freshly ground pepper

Have fish retailer prepare oysters on-the-half-shell or, working over a bowl to catch liquor, open oysters. Reserve any oyster liquor; strain through several layers of cheesecloth to remove bits of shell or debris. Preheat oven to 450F (230C). Spread rock salt to a depth of 1/2 inch in a shallow baking pan large enough to hold oyster shells in a single layer. Place pan in oven. In a large skillet, melt butter or margarine over medium heat. Add shallots, fennel or tarragon and parsley; sauté 4 to 5 minutes. Add watercress or spinach; cook until limp. Pour mixture into a blender or food processor fitted with a metal blade. Add liqueur and 1 tablespoon reserved oyster liquor. Process until smooth; season with salt and pepper to taste. Cool slightly. Spoon mixture over each oyster, spreading to cover. Remove baking pan from oven; nestle oyster shells in hot salt. Return baking pan to oven. Bake 4 to 5 minutes or until hot and bubbling. Serve immediately. Makes 4 to 6 appetizer servings.

Chilled Scallops with Chive Sauce

Chilled scallops served in scallop shells make an elegant and beautiful presentation.

1/2 cup Mayonnaise, page 144,
   or other mayonnaise
1-1/2 tablespoons lime juice
Pinch of white pepper
1 lb. scallops

1 tablespoon butter
3 tablespoons finely chopped chives
Lime slices
Watercress or parsley sprigs

In a small bowl, whisk together mayonnaise, lime juice and white pepper; set aside. If using large sea scallops, cut into thirds; leave bay scallops whole. Melt butter in a large skillet. Add whole or cut scallops; sauté 1 to 2 minutes or until firm and opaque. Do not overcook. Use a slotted spoon to place sautéed scallops in a medium bowl. Cook juices remaining in skillet until reduced almost to a jelly-like consistency. Remove skillet from heat; whisk in mayonnaise mixture and 2 tablespoons chives. Gently stir sauce into scallops. Refrigerate until chilled. Serve in individual dishes or scallop shells. Sprinkle with remaining chives; garnish with lime slices and watercress or parsley sprigs. Makes 6 appetizer servings.

Large scallop shells—real or made from porcelain—are often used for cooking and serving scallops. They can be purchased at kitchenware shops and are attractive for presenting all kinds of shellfish.

How to Make Oysters Rockefeller

1/Spoon watercress or spinach mixture over oysters in shells.

2/Nestle oyster shells in hot salt. Bake until hot and bubbly.

Smoked-Trout Pâté   Photo on page 125.

Use a blender or food processor to make this smooth, rich appetizer.

1 to 1-1/4 lbs. smoked trout
   (3 medium trout)
1 (3 oz.) pkg. cream cheese,
   room temperature
About 1/4 cup whipping cream
2 to 3 teaspoons prepared horseradish
2 tablespoons lemon juice

2 green onions, chopped
5 or 6 parsley sprigs
1 tablespoon finely chopped dill or
   1 teaspoon dill weed, if desired
Lemon slices, if desired
Parsley sprigs, if desired
Crackers or cucumber slices

Skin, bone and flake trout. In a blender or food processor fitted with a metal blade, puree flaked trout, cream cheese, 1/4 cup whipping cream, horseradish, lemon juice, green onions, parsley and dill, if desired. Add more cream, if necessary, to make a spreadable mixture. Spoon trout mixture into a serving bowl. Cover and refrigerate until served. To serve, bring mixture to room temperature. Garnish with lemon slices and parsley, if desired. Serve as a spread for crackers or cucumber slices. Makes 2 cups.

Prawns Pacifica

A great do-ahead party dish because the shrimp marinate overnight.

Water
Salt
1-1/2 lbs. medium shrimp
1 medium onion, thinly sliced,
  separated into rings
1/2 cup cider vinegar
1/4 cup ketchup
2 tablespoons sugar
1 tablespoon finely chopped parsley
1 garlic clove, minced
1 teaspoon salt
1 teaspoon mustard seeds
1/2 teaspoon celery seeds
1/4 teaspoon red (cayenne) pepper
1/8 teaspoon black pepper
1/2 cup vegetable oil
3 medium oranges, peeled
Spinach or chicory leaves

In a large saucepan, bring lightly salted water to a boil. Add shrimp; cook 2 to 3 minutes or until shrimp become firm and turn pink. Immerse in cold water to stop cooking. Remove shells; devein, if desired. In a large bowl, combine shelled shrimp and onion. In a small bowl, combine vinegar, ketchup, sugar, parsley, garlic, salt, mustard seeds, celery seeds, red pepper and black pepper. Add oil; beat with a whisk to combine. Pour dressing over shrimp. Cover; refrigerate at least 12 hours, stirring once or twice. Cut each orange into 3 or 4 slices. Cut each slice into quarters; add to shrimp mixture. Toss to distribute and coat with marinade; drain off marinade. Line a platter or bowl with spinach or chicory leaves. Mound shrimp mixture onto leaves. Serve as an appetizer. Makes 6 to 8 servings.

Mussels Vinaigrette

Glossy black-shell mussels, lemons and onions create a beautiful array of colors and textures.

30 small mussels (about 1-1/2 lbs.)
Dry white wine
1/3 cup olive oil or vegetable oil
1/4 teaspoon salt
1/8 teaspoon pepper
1/4 teaspoon sugar
1 large garlic clove, minced
1/4 cup finely chopped parsley
1 small white onion, thinly sliced,
  separated into rings
1 lemon, thinly sliced

Scrub mussels with a brush to remove dirt from shells. Remove beards; discard any mussels that do not close. Place mussels in a kettle; add enough wine to measure 1 inch in bottom of kettle. Bring wine to a simmer. Cover and cook 5 to 7 minutes or until mussels open. Turn mussels after 3 minutes. With a slotted spoon, transfer mussels in their shells to a 13'' x 9'' glass baking dish. Discard any cooked mussels that do not open. Boil cooking liquid in kettle until reduced to about 1/2 cup. In a small bowl, whisk together 1/4 cup reduced cooking liquid, oil, salt, pepper, sugar, garlic and parsley. Pour over hot mussels. Add sliced onion and lemon; toss gently. Cover and refrigerate at least 6 hours, turning mussels once or twice and spooning marinade into shells. Let chilled cooked mussels stand at room temperature 30 minutes before serving. Makes 4 to 6 main-dish servings.

Sardines in Dill Sauce   Photo on page 125.

Sardine fans will relish this appetizer.

3 (3-3/4-oz.) cans oil-pack Norwegian
   bristling sardines
1/4 cup lemon juice
2 tablespoons Dijon-style mustard
3 tablespoons vegetable oil or
   light olive oil
2-1/4 teaspoons white-wine vinegar
1 teaspoon sugar

1/4 cup chopped dill or
   1-1/2 tablespoons dill weed
1-1/2 tablespoons finely chopped parsley
1/8 teaspoon salt
Lettuce leaves
Cherry tomatoes, if desired
1 baguette French bread or black bread,
   sliced, buttered

Drain sardines. Place in a shallow bowl; cover with half of the lemon juice. Cover bowl; refrigerate at least 2 hours. Pour mustard into a small bowl. Use a fork to gradually beat oil into mustard until creamy. Beat in vinegar, sugar, dill, parsley, salt and remaining lemon juice. Line a serving dish with lettuce leaves. Drain sardines; arrange over lettuce. Spoon sauce over sardines. Garnish with cherry tomatoes, if desired. Serve slightly chilled or at room temperature with buttered bread. Makes 8 to 12 appetizer servings.

Bagna Cauda

Cream mellows the garlic in this vegetable dip.

1/2 cup butter or margarine
10 to 12 garlic cloves, minced
1 (2-oz.) can flat anchovies, rinsed,
   drained, chopped
1 cup half and half
1/2 cup whipping cream
Italian or French bread, thinly sliced

Carrot and celery sticks, cherry tomatoes,
   mushroom caps, blanched green beans,
   cooked artichoke leaves, cabbage wedges,
   red- or green-bell-pepper strips,
   zucchini slices, yellow-squash or
   Jerusalem-artichoke slices
   (1/2 to 3/4 cup per person)

In a medium saucepan, melt 1/4 cup butter or margarine over low heat. Add garlic; sauté about 1 minute. Add anchovies. Stirring frequently, cook until anchovies dissolve into a paste. Add remaining 1/4 cup butter or margarine, half and half and whipping cream. Cook over low heat about 15 minutes or until mixture reduces to about 1-3/4 cups and is thick enough to coat a spoon. Pour into a fondue or other pot; keep warm over an alcohol flame or candle warmer. Serve warm with a basket of bread and a selection of raw vegetables. Guests can dip vegetables in sauce, then hold a slice of bread under vegetables to catch any dribbles. Makes about 1-3/4 cups.

To get the most flavor from dried herbs, crush them in the palm of your hand.

Terrine de Coquilles

This superb terrine will be a hit at a cocktail buffet or served as an elegant first course.

1 lb. skinless lingcod, whiting,
   red snapper, cod, turbot, pompano or
   other lean white fish fillets
	1/4 teaspoon paprika
	1-1/2 cups whipping cream
	Pernod Mayonnaise, page 144

2 lbs. scallops	Chives, if desired
2 egg whites	Watercress, parsley or dill sprigs
1 teaspoon salt	Cooked carrot slices, cut in flowers,
1/4 teaspoon white pepper	if desired, or cherry tomatoes

Preheat oven to 350F (175C). Butter a rectangular 1-quart terrine or 8" x 5" loaf pan; set aside. Cut fillets into large pieces. Reserve half of scallops. In a blender or food processor fitted with a metal blade, puree fish and remaining half of scallops. Add egg whites, salt, white pepper and paprika. Process several seconds until blended. With machine running, slowly add cream until thoroughly blended. Spoon half of fish paste into buttered terrine or loaf pan; spread evenly. Tap container on counter once or twice to remove any air bubbles. Arrange reserved scallops on top. Spread remaining fish paste over scallops; smooth top. Tap container on counter again. Butter a sheet of parchment or waxed paper; place on surface of fish mixture. Set terrine or pan in a large baking pan; place on oven rack. Pour boiling water into outer baking pan to a depth of 1 to 2 inches. Bake 30 to 40 minutes or until a knife inserted in center comes out clean. Remove terrine from water bath. Cool on a wire rack to room temperature, draining off any liquid that accumulates in terrine. Prepare Pernod Mayonnaise. When terrine is cool, invert onto a serving plate. Frost top and sides of terrine with a thin layer of Pernod Mayonnaise. Arrange chives in a lattice pattern on top, if desired. Garnish with watercress, parsley or dill, and carrot flowers or cherry tomatoes. Serve remaining Pernod Mayonnaise separately. Makes 10 to 12 appetizer servings.

Taramasalata

Serve in a hollowed-out eggplant for a dramatic presentation.

2 (1-oz.) slices French bread,
   crusts removed, or
   white sandwich bread
	1 green onion, chopped
	1 cup light olive oil
	Freshly ground pepper

2 (2-oz.) jars salmon caviar	Finely chopped parsley
1 egg	Greek olives, if desired
2 tablespoons lemon juice	Pita bread

In a blender or food processor fitted with a metal blade, process bread, 1 jar caviar, egg, lemon juice and onion until blended. With machine running, slowly pour in oil, processing until thick and creamy. Season with pepper to taste. Spoon into a small serving bowl. Refrigerate dip to chill slightly before serving. Sprinkle with parsley; garnish with remaining caviar and olives, if desired. Cut pita bread into triangles; lightly toast. Serve dip with toasted pita triangles. Makes about 2 cups.

Clockwise from top: Beer-Boiled Shrimp, page 43; Smoked-Trout Pâté, page 121; Smoked-Salmon Spread, page 128; Sardines in Dill Sauce, page 123; Terrine de Coquilles, above; Taramasalata, above.

Coquilles Saint Jacques Nouvelle

A simple, light approach to delicate scallops.

1 lb. scallops
1/2 cup dry white wine
1 cup whipping cream
3 tablespoons butter
2 shallots or 1 green onion,
  white portion only, finely chopped

1/2 lb. mushrooms, sliced
1 large bunch spinach, stems removed
1/4 cup water
Salt
White pepper
Finely chopped parsley or chives

If using large sea scallops, cut into halves or thirds; leave bay scallops whole. In a medium saucepan, heat wine to simmering. Add scallops; simmer 1 minute or until scallops become firm and opaque. Use a slotted spoon to remove cooked scallops from pan; set aside. Cook wine over medium-high heat until reduced to 2 tablespoons. Stir in cream. Stirring occasionally, cook until sauce is reduced to about 3/4 cup; set aside. Melt 2 tablespoons butter in a large skillet. Add shallots or green onion and mushrooms; sauté 5 to 6 minutes. Set aside. Stack 10 to 12 spinach leaves on top of one another; roll lengthwise, jelly-roll fashion. Cut crosswise into 1/2-inch slices. Repeat with remaining leaves. In a large skillet, bring remaining 1 tablespoon butter and water to a simmer. Add spinach; cook 30 seconds or until spinach is tender. Drain; season with salt and white pepper to taste. Spoon evenly onto individual serving plates or scallop shells. Reheat cream sauce; add cooked scallops and sautéed mixture; stirring occasionally, heat through. Spoon hot scallop mixture onto cooked spinach. Garnish with parsley or chives. Makes 6 to 8 appetizer servings or 4 main-dish servings.

Hot Crab Spread

A rich and inviting appetizer served piping hot.

2 (3-oz.) pkgs. cream cheese,
  room temperature
2 tablespoons Mayonnaise, page 144,
  or other mayonnaise
1-1/2 tablespoons lemon juice
1 tablespoon dry sherry

3/4 to 1 teaspoon curry powder
Pinch of sugar
1 (6-oz.) can crabmeat, drained
Salt and pepper
1 small green onion, sliced
Crackers or 1 baguette French bread, sliced

Preheat oven to 350F (175C). In a medium bowl, combine cream cheese, mayonnaise, lemon juice, sherry, curry powder and sugar; stir to blend. Flake crabmeat; remove cartilage. Gently fold crabmeat into cream-cheese mixture. Season with salt and pepper to taste. Spoon crab mixture into an ovenproof serving dish. Bake 10 to 15 minutes or until heated through. Scatter green onion over top. Serve hot with crackers or bread. Makes 1-1/2 cups.

There is a voluntary government inspection program for prepackaged seafood, but most fresh fish and shellfish are not government inspected. Your best insurance of quality is to deal with a reputable fish market.

Tapenade

A tempting spread that is easy to make with canned fish.

1 (6-1/2-oz.) can oil-pack tuna
3 or 4 anchovy fillets, drained
1/4 cup Mayonnaise, page 144,
  or other mayonnaise
2 parsley sprigs

1 green onion, chopped
1 tablespoon lemon juice
Freshly ground pepper
Crackers or 1 baguette French bread, sliced

In a blender or food processor fitted with a metal blade, puree tuna with oil, anchovies, mayonnaise, parsley, green onion and lemon juice. Season with pepper to taste. Spoon into a small serving bowl. Serve with crackers or bread. Makes 1-1/4 cups.

Tuna Dip Mexicana

Here's a spirited party dip that can be prepared quickly.

1 (6-1/2-oz.) can oil- or
  water-pack tuna, drained
1 green onion, chopped
3 tablespoons canned diced green chilies or
  chopped fresh green chilies
  to taste

1/4 cup Mayonnaise, page 144,
  or other mayonnaise
6 to 8 cilantro sprigs, chopped
Lime or lemon juice
Salt and pepper
Tortilla chips

In a medium bowl, combine tuna, green onion, chilies and mayonnaise. Stir in cilantro. Season with lime or lemon juice. Add salt and pepper to taste. Serve with chips. Makes about 1-1/3 cups.

Dill-Shrimp Spread

Try this delicate spread on small biscuits, slivers of French bread or tiny crackers.

1/4 cup butter, room temperature
1/2 (8-oz.) pkg. cream cheese,
  room temperature
1/2 lb. tiny, shelled, cooked shrimp or
  2 (4-oz.) cans tiny shrimp

Finely chopped dill sprigs or dill weed
Dry sherry
Salt

In a blender or food processor fitted with a metal blade, process butter and cream cheese until smooth. If using canned shrimp, rinse and drain thoroughly. Add shrimp to cream-cheese mixture. Process until smooth. Add dill, sherry and salt to taste. Serve as a spread. Makes about 1-1/2 cups.

Smoked-Salmon Spread   Photo on page 125.

So easy to make for breakfast or brunch, and tasty in sandwiches or on bagels.

1 (8 oz.) pkg. cream cheese,
    room temperature
1 tablespoon lemon juice

2 tablespoons milk
4 oz. smoked salmon
Lemon or lime wedges

In a blender or food processor fitted with a metal blade, puree cream cheese, lemon juice, milk and 3 ounces smoked salmon until smooth. Add remaining salmon; turn machine on and off until mixture is blended but bits of salmon remain. *Do not puree.* Spoon into a serving bowl; garnish with lemon or lime wedges. Serve as a spread. Makes 1-1/2 cups.

Smoky Salmon Spread

Economical canned salmon and a few drops of liquid smoke taste similar to smoked salmon.

1 (16-oz.) can red salmon
2 (3-oz.) pkgs. cream cheese,
    room temperature
2 or 3 dill sprigs or
    3/4 to 1 teaspoon dill weed

1 teaspoon lemon juice
1/2 teaspoon natural-hickory liquid smoke
Few drops hot-pepper sauce
Chopped chives or parsley
Crackers or bagels, split, toasted, buttered

Drain salmon, reserving 1 tablespoon salmon liquid; flake salmon. In a blender or food processor fitted with a metal blade, process flaked salmon and reserved liquid, cream cheese, dill, lemon juice, liquid smoke and hot-pepper sauce until smooth. Spoon into a serving bowl. Cover and refrigerate at least 2 hours to let flavors blend. Garnish with chives or parsley. Serve as a spread with crackers or bagels. Makes about 1 cup.

Smoked Salmon

- **Kippered salmon, Scotch-smoked salmon, lox** and **nova** or **Nova Scotia salmon,** are all forms of smoked salmon.
- **Kippered salmon** is a mildly brined and smoke-cooked fillet, chunk or steak. Most kippered salmon is made from chinook salmon that is dyed red before smoking.
- **Scotch-smoked salmon** refers to cold-smoked Atlantic salmon, not **smoked salmon** which is cold-smoked from the Pacific chinook or coho species. Cold-smoking does not cook the fish.
- **Lox** is the name for mildly brined, cold-smoked salmon. It is popular served with cream cheese and bagels.
- **Nova** or **Nova Scotia salmon,** a popular deli item, is a New York idiom for a type of cold-smoked salmon.

Seviche

The lime-juice marinade changes the texture and literally cooks the fish.

1 lb. firm-texture, skinless red snapper,
   rock cod, halibut or
   other lean white fish fillets
1/4 cup fresh lime juice (2 limes)
1 large tomato, seeded, diced
1 avocado, diced
3 green onions, thinly sliced
1/2 cup sliced ripe olives
About 1 tablespoon finely chopped,
   fresh or canned green chilies

2 garlic cloves, minced
2 tablespoons olive oil
1 to 2 teaspoons finely chopped cilantro
1-1/2 teaspoons finely chopped oregano or
   1/2 teaspoon dried leaf oregano
Salt
Freshly ground pepper
Cilantro leaves

Cut fish into 1/2-inch pieces; place in a deep bowl. Pour lime juice over fish pieces. Cover and re-frigerate at least 3 hours, stirring once or twice. Drain fish; stir in tomato, avocado, green onions, olives, chilies, garlic, oil, chopped cilantro and oregano. Season with salt and pepper to taste. Garnish with cilantro leaves. Makes 6 to 8 appetizer servings.

Pickled Herring

What a heavenly flavor from such a simple process!

1 lb. herring, cleaned, scaled
2 cups white vinegar
1 cup water
1-1/2 tablespoons pickling spices

1 bay leaf
2 tablespoons sugar
1 onion, sliced, separated into rings

Remove heads and tails from herring. Rinse fish; pat dry with paper towels. In a medium saucepan, combine vinegar, water, pickling spices, bay leaf and sugar. Bring to a boil; cool to room temperature. Slice rinsed fish crosswise into 1-1/2- to 2-inch pieces. Arrange herring and onion rings in alternate layers in a 1-quart jar or tall, narrow container with a tight-fitting lid. Pour pickling liquid over herring and onion rings. Add water to completely cover, if necessary. Cover jar or container; refrigerate 5 to 7 days before serving. Makes 1 quart.

Fresh herring is soft-textured, but becomes firm when pickled or smoked. For names of commercially pre-pared herring, see page 15.

Brunch, Lunch & Supper Dishes

This chapter features a variety of dishes that can be prepared for lunch, brunch or a light supper. The recipes are perfect for casual weekend meals, picnics and informal entertaining.

Brunch is an ideal time to entertain. There are no rules that tell you what to serve. The food can be simple, but is generally more substantial than breakfast. Brunch Crab Soufflé is the dish for late-risers. It's prepared the evening before, refrigerated, then baked in the morning. Hangtown Fry takes the form of an omelet or scrambled eggs. Prepare it seconds before serving. Harborside Hash transforms last night's leftovers into a hearty dish for breakfast or lunch.

Eggs Benedict takes on a new flavor with smoked salmon instead of ham or Canadian bacon. And don't miss out on Gravlax, a Scandinavian preparation of raw salmon cured with salt, sugar and dill. Serve paper-thin slices accompanied by a tangy Mustard-Dill Sauce. Or, serve Gravlax for brunch with softly scrambled eggs and a croissant.

Pasta, always perfect for supper, takes on a new slant with California-Style Pasta. It is an innovative combination of fettucini, smoked salmon, grapes and pistachios in a light cream-cheese sauce. From the heart of Sicily comes Spaghetti Salsa Verde—spaghetti tossed with a robust sauce of fresh basil, anchovies and tuna.

Be adventurous! Make up your own pasta-and-seafood dishes. Stuff large cooked pasta shells with tasty combinations of crabmeat or shrimp and mushrooms. Add some chopped green onions and a mild sauce to bind the mixture. Or, add flaked cooked fish, such as sole, flounder or tuna, to a traditional macaroni salad. Serve with a tangy sauce.

Sandwiches are always a good standby for lunch or supper. Curried-Tuna Muffin and Niçoise Sandwich are a cut above everyday fare. And for a cozy Sunday supper, try Toasted Crab Rolls or Salmon Melt with a mug of soup.

Niçoise Sandwich

A fresh idea—a niçoise salad in a crusty French roll.

6 (5- to 6-inch) French sandwich rolls
2 tablespoons red-wine vinegar
1 garlic clove, minced
3/4 cup olive oil
Salt and black pepper
2-1/2 cups torn romaine lettuce
1 (6-1/2-oz.) can oil-pack albacore
 tuna, undrained
1 small green bell pepper,
 cut in thin strips

10 Italian or Greek black olives,
 pitted, quartered
1 (2-oz.) can flat anchovies,
 drained, chopped
1 tablespoon drained capers
2 to 3 tablespoons chopped basil, if desired
1 large tomato, thinly sliced
2 hard-cooked eggs, thinly sliced

Split each roll in half lengthwise; pull out some of center of each roll. In a small bowl, blend vinegar, garlic and oil. Add salt and black pepper to taste. Brush hollowed-out rolls with some of vinegar mixture. In a medium bowl, combine remaining ingredients. Gently toss with remaining vinegar mixture. Fill rolls with salad mixture. Makes 6 sandwiches.

Toasted Crab Rolls

Serve these Gruyère-and-crabmeat sandwiches for a special Sunday-night treat.

4 or 5 (5- to 6-inch) French sandwich rolls
1/4 cup butter or margarine, melted
3/4 lb. fresh crabmeat
1 cup shredded Gruyère cheese (4 oz.)
2 green onions, chopped
2 tablespoons dairy sour cream

1/4 cup Mayonnaise, page 144,
 or other mayonnaise
Lemon juice to taste
Salt and pepper
Ground nutmeg, if desired

Split rolls in half lengthwise. Brush with butter or margarine. In a large skillet, lightly toast rolls. Preheat oven to 400F (205C). Flake crabmeat; remove cartilage. In a medium bowl, combine flaked crabmeat, cheese, green onions, sour cream and mayonnaise. Season to taste with lemon juice, salt, pepper and nutmeg, if desired. Spoon crab mixture onto half the split toasted rolls. Place on a baking sheet. Bake 5 to 10 minutes or until sandwiches are hot. Serve with other half of roll to side. Makes 4 or 5 sandwiches.

Salmon Melt

A terrific sandwich for a casual supper or informal gathering.

2 English muffins
1 (7-3/4-oz.) can pink salmon
Milk
1 tablespoon butter or margarine
1 tablespoon all-purpose flour
1/4 teaspoon dill weed
1/8 teaspoon salt
1 egg yolk

1/4 cup finely chopped celery
1 tablespoon finely chopped
   pimiento-stuffed-olives
4 tomato slices
1/4 cup freshly grated Parmesan cheese
   (3/4 oz.)
Pimiento-stuffed-olive slices

Preheat broiler. Split English muffins; place on a broiling pan. Toast split muffins in broiler; set aside. Drain salmon, reserving liquid in a 1-cup measure. Add milk to liquid to make 1/2 cup. Flake salmon; set aside. Melt butter or margarine in a small saucepan. Stir in flour, dill and salt. Slowly stir in milk mixture. Stirring constantly, cook until smooth and slightly thickened. In a small bowl, beat egg yolk; blend in 1/4 cup sauce. Stir egg-yolk mixture into remaining sauce; heat through. *Do not boil.* Remove pan from heat; fold in flaked salmon, celery and chopped olives. Place a tomato slice on each split, toasted muffin half. Spoon salmon mixture over tomato slices. Sprinkle with cheese. Broil sandwiches until tops are lightly browned. Garnish with olive slices. Makes 4 open-face sandwiches.

Variation

Substitute 1 (6-1/2-ounce) can oil- or water-pack albacore tuna for salmon.

Spaghetti Salsa Verde

Take advantage of fresh basil in season with this robust Sicilian pasta dish.

2 cups tightly packed basil leaves
2 cups loosely packed parsley sprigs
2 garlic cloves
1 (2-oz.) can flat anchovies,
   rinsed, drained
3/4 cup olive oil
1/4 cup butter or margarine,
   room temperature

2 to 3 tablespoons lemon juice
1/8 teaspoon freshly ground pepper
2 (6-1/2-oz.) cans water-pack albacore
   tuna, drained
1 lb. thin spaghetti, uncooked
Freshly grated Parmesan cheese, if desired

In a blender or food processor fitted with a metal blade, process basil, parsley and garlic until finely chopped. Add anchovies, 1/2 cup oil, butter or margarine, lemon juice and pepper. Puree to a smooth paste. Finely flake tuna into a large bowl. Gently fold in basil mixture. Let stand while cooking spaghetti. Cook spaghetti according to package directions. Drain; rinse under cold running water. Drain again. Return to kettle; add remaining 1/4 cup oil. Heat spaghetti, tossing with oil, until pasta is hot. Add tuna mixture to spaghetti mixture; toss to distribute. Spoon into a large serving bowl. Serve immediately. Serve Parmesan cheese separately, if desired. Makes 6 servings.

How to Make Crab Tostadas

1/Holding a ladle in center of tortilla to form a cup, fry in hot oil until crisp and golden brown. Drain on paper towels.

2/Spoon crab mixture into center of tortilla cups. Top each with tomatoes, avocado, olives, cheese and a dollop of sour cream.

Smoked-Salmon Benedict

Smoked salmon instead of ham in Eggs Benedict? It's delightful!

**Basic or Blender Hollandaise Sauce,
    page 154**
3 English muffins, split
Butter or margarine
6 to 9 thin smoked-salmon slices

6 large eggs
Salt and pepper
**Salmon caviar or
    finely chopped ripe olives, if desired**

Prepare Basic or Blender Hollandaise Sauce; keep warm over hot water. Do not let water come to a simmer. Toast muffin halves; butter lightly. Place smoked-salmon slices on top of buttered muffin halves. In a medium saucepan or skillet, pour water 1-1/2 to 2 inches deep. Bring to a boil; reduce to a simmer. Break each egg into a small bowl. Slip eggs into water, one at a time, holding bowl close to surface of water. Poach eggs 3 to 5 minutes. Use a slotted spoon to lift poached eggs from water. Place 1 egg on each salmon-topped muffin half. Season with salt and pepper. Spoon Basic or Blender Hollandaise Sauce over top. Garnish with a small amount of caviar or olives, if desired. Makes 6 servings.

Crab Tostadas

The unusual flour-tortilla serving cups are easily made using a wok and ladle.

Oil for deep-frying
4 (9-inch) flour tortillas
3 tablespoons Mayonnaise, page 144,
  or other mayonnaise
3 tablespoons dairy sour cream
2 to 3 teaspoons mild green taco sauce,
  or to taste
1/2 lb. fresh crabmeat or
  1 (6-oz.) can crabmeat, drained
3 cups shredded lettuce

3 or 4 green onions, sliced
1 tomato, diced
1 avocado, diced
1/3 cup sliced ripe olives
1/2 cup shredded Monterey Jack or
  Cheddar cheese (2 oz.)
Dairy sour cream
Mild green taco sauce, if desired

Pour oil 2 to 3 inches deep into a wok, deep-fryer or heavy saucepan. Heat to 370F (190C) or until a 1-inch cube of bread turns golden brown in 50 seconds. Holding a ladle in center of tortilla to form a cup, fry 1 tortilla in hot oil until crisp and golden brown. Drain on paper towels; repeat with remaining tortillas. In a small bowl, combine mayonnaise, sour cream and 2 to 3 teaspoons taco sauce or to taste. Flake crabmeat into a separate bowl; remove cartilage. Add shredded lettuce and green onions. Toss mayonnaise mixture with crab mixture. Spoon crab mixture into center of tortilla cups. Top each with a sprinkling of tomato, avocado, olives and cheese. Spoon a dollop of sour cream on top of each. Serve with additional taco sauce, if desired. Makes 4 servings.

Smoked-Salmon Sandwich

This makes a perfect picnic or party meal when served with chilled fruit and a beverage.

Smoked-Salmon Spread, page 128
1/2 small red onion, thinly sliced,
  separated into rings
Ice water

1 (1-lb.) baguette French bread
1 tomato, thinly sliced
3/4 to 1 cup thin cucumber slices
1-1/2 teaspoons drained capers

Prepare Smoked-Salmon Spread; set aside. In a small bowl, soak onion rings in ice water 15 minutes. Drain; pat dry with paper towels. Split bread lengthwise, but do not cut through. Open carefully; pull out center of loaf, leaving a 1/2-inch shell. Spread salmon mixture evenly into halves. Layer tomato slices over bottom half of loaf. Top with cucumber slices, then drained onion rings and capers. Close sandwich and gently press together. Secure with wooden skewers or picks. To serve, cut diagonally into slices. Makes 4 to 6 servings.

Gravlax

For breakfast, serve Gravlax with softly scrambled eggs and croissants.

About 3 lbs. center-cut salmon
1 large bunch dill sprigs
1/4 cup coarse salt or kosher salt
1/4 cup sugar

1 tablespoon white peppercorns, crushed
Mustard-Dill Sauce, page 145
Dill sprigs or lemon wedges

Leaving skin on, cut salmon into 2 boneless fillets. To fillet, cut down center back, then on both sides of backbone. Cut flesh from backbone and ribs. Discard bones or use to make Fish Stock. Rinse boned fish; pat dry with paper towels. Run your fingers over boned area; remove any small bones. Lay 1 fillet, skin-side down, in a 13" x 9" glass or porcelain dish. Spread dill over fillet. In a small bowl, combine salt, sugar and crushed peppercorns. Sprinkle over dill. Top with other fillet, skin-side up. Place thick part of upper fillet to thin part of lower fillet. This makes thickness more even. Cover dish with foil; weight down with another baking dish of similar size and a 5-pound weight or several cans of food. Refrigerate 48 to 72 hours. Every 12 hours, turn salmon and baste with accumulated juices. Prepare Mustard-Dill Sauce. To serve, remove fillets from marinade, scraping away dill and seasonings. Rinse if too salty; pat dry. With skin-side down, slice salmon flesh thinly on the diagonal, removing from skin. To serve, arrange on a platter, overlapping slices, or roll each slice. Garnish with dill sprigs or lemon wedges. Serve with Mustard-Dill Sauce. Makes 8 to 12 servings.

Hangtown Fry

This California gold-rush favorite is popular today for breakfast or brunch.

1 (8- or 10-oz.) jar shucked oysters,
    drained
Salt and pepper
All-purpose flour
10 eggs

Water
3/4 cup finely crushed saltine crackers
1/4 cup milk
3 tablespoons butter or margarine
Crisp-fried bacon slices

If oysters are large, cut in half. Season lightly with salt and pepper. Roll each oyster in flour to coat lightly. In a shallow dish, beat 1 egg with 1 tablespoon water. Dip oysters in egg mixture, then roll in cracker crumbs to coat. In a medium bowl, beat together remaining eggs, milk, salt and pepper. *To make 2 omelets:* For each omelet, melt half the butter or margarine in a 10-inch skillet. Add half the coated oysters; brown quickly over medium-high heat. Do not overcook. Pour half the egg mixture over oysters in skillet. Reduce heat to low; cook until egg mixture is set. During cooking, lift cooked egg mixture with a spatula and let uncooked egg mixture run underneath. To serve, fold omelet in half; turn out onto a platter. Serve with bacon. Repeat with remaining oysters and eggs. *To scramble eggs:* Melt butter or margarine in a large skillet. Add coated oysters; brown quickly over medium-high heat. Do not overcook. Pour egg mixture over oysters in skillet. Reduce heat to medium-low; softly scramble eggs. Spoon cooked eggs and oysters onto a platter. Serve with bacon. Makes 4 to 6 servings.

How to Make Gravlax

1/Lay half of fish in a single layer, skin-side down, in a glass or porcelain dish. Top with dill and salt mixture.

2/Thinly slice salmon on the diagonal, removing from skin. Serve slices overlapped or rolled.

Harborside Hash

Turn last night's leftovers into hearty breakfast fare.

4 bacon slices
1 small onion, chopped
2 cups cooked, flaked fish
2 cups cooked, peeled, diced potatoes
1 to 2 tablespoons chopped parsley
3/4 teaspoon finely chopped thyme or
** 1/4 teaspoon dried leaf thyme, crumbled**

3/4 to 1 teaspoon finely chopped rosemary
** or 1/4 to 1/2 teaspoon dried leaf**
** rosemary, crumbled**
1/2 teaspoon Worcestershire sauce
Salt and pepper
Fresh Mexican Salsa, page 150, ketchup or
** chili sauce, if desired**

In a large skillet, cook bacon until crisp. Drain on paper towels. Reserve about 3 tablespoons bacon drippings in skillet. Add onion; sauté until soft and transparent. Add fish, potatoes, parsley, thyme, rosemary and Worcestershire sauce. Add salt and pepper to taste. Stirring constantly, cook over medium-high heat until mixture starts to brown. Serve from skillet or spoon into a large serving bowl. Crumble bacon; scatter over hash. Serve hot with Fresh Mexican Salsa, ketchup or chili sauce, if desired. Makes 4 servings.

Shrimp Curry with Orange Rice

An array of condiments adds interest to this curry dish.

Orange Rice, see below
Water
Salt
1-1/2 lbs. medium or large shrimp
1/2 cup butter or margarine
1/3 cup all-purpose flour
1-1/2 to 2 tablespoons finely shredded
  gingerroot

2-1/2 to 3 teaspoons curry powder,
  more if desired
2-3/4 cups half and half
4 teaspoons lemon juice, or to taste
1 tablespoon dry sherry, or to taste
Pepper

Condiments:
Chopped green onions
Dry-roasted peanuts
Toasted shredded coconut
Raisins

Chutney
Diced apple
Chopped crystallized ginger

Orange Rice:
2-1/2 cups water
1-1/2 tablespoons finely shredded orange peel
3/4 cup freshly squeezed orange juice

2 tablespoons butter or margarine
3/4 teaspoon salt
1-1/2 cups uncooked long-grain white rice

Prepare Orange Rice. In a large saucepan, bring lightly salted water to a boil. Add shrimp; cook 2 to 3 minutes or until firm and pink. Shell and devein shrimp; set aside. Melt butter or margarine in a large saucepan. Stir in flour, gingerroot and curry. Stirring constantly, cook until mixture is smooth and bubbly. Gradually stir in half and half, lemon juice and sherry. Season with salt and pepper to taste. Add cooked, shelled shrimp; heat through. Serve curry with Orange Rice and your choice of condiments. Makes 6 servings.

Orange Rice:
In a medium saucepan, combine water, orange peel, orange juice, butter or margarine and salt. Bring liquid to a boil. Stir in rice. Reduce heat; cover and simmer 20 minutes or until all liquid has been absorbed. Uncover; let stand 5 minutes before serving. Makes about 4-1/2 cups.

Curried-Tuna Muffin

This sandwich filling is tasty on raisin toast, too.

3 raisin English muffins
1 (6-1/2-oz.) can oil- or
  water-pack albacore tuna, drained
1/4 cup slivered almonds, toasted
1-1/2 to 2 tablespoons chutney,
  coarsely chopped

1 small green onion, chopped
2 tablespoons Mayonnaise, page 144,
  or other mayonnaise
1/4 teaspoon curry powder, or to taste
Lemon juice to taste

Split English muffins; toast each half. In a medium bowl, combine remaining ingredients. Spoon mixture onto toasted muffin halves. Makes 6 open-face sandwiches.

Shrimp Curry with Orange Rice

California-Style Pasta

Melt-in-your-mouth goodness accented with bits of pistachios for color and flavor.

1/2 cup dry-roasted, shelled pistachios
1/4 cup butter or margarine
3 green onions
1 large garlic clove, minced
1-1/2 cups half and half
6 oz. cream cheese, room temperature,
  cut in chunks
About 3/4 teaspoon finely shredded lemon peel
1-1/2 to 2 teaspoons lemon juice

White pepper
Salt
Water
3/4 lb. fresh fettucini or
  1 (8- or 10-oz.) pkg. dried fettucini
1 cup seedless green grapes, cut in half
6 oz. thinly sliced smoked salmon,
  cut in 1/2-inch squares

Rub pistachios against each other to remove most of skins and expose green interior. In a small skillet, melt 1 tablespoon butter or margarine. Add skinned pistachios; sauté until toasted. Be careful because pistachios burn easily; set aside. Slice green onions, separating white portions from green tops. Set sliced green-onion tops aside. Melt remaining 3 tablespoons butter or margarine in a medium saucepan. Add sliced white portions of green-onions and garlic; sauté until onion is soft and transparent. Add half and half and cream cheese. Stirring constantly, cook over medium-low heat until cheese melts and sauce is smooth. Remove from heat. Season with lemon peel, lemon juice and white pepper to taste. Salt lightly, if desired; most smoked salmon is salty. Bring a large kettle of salted water to a rapid boil; add fresh or packaged pasta. Cook fresh pasta about 3 minutes; cook packaged pasta according to package directions. Drain and return to kettle. Add cream sauce; toss to distribute. Reserve about 1/4 each of toasted pistachios, grapes and green-onion tops for garnish. Add remaining toasted pistachios, grapes, green-onion tops and salmon to pasta mixture. Adjust seasonings to taste. Pour onto a platter or into a large serving bowl. To serve, garnish with reserved pistachios, green-onion tops and grapes. Makes 5 or 6 servings.

Fish Mousse

Leftover fish is delicious prepared in this lovely dish.

1/2 cup cold water
2 teaspoons unflavored gelatin
3/4 cup Mayonnaise, page 144, or
  other mayonnaise
1 cup cooked, flaked fish (about 6 oz.)
1/2 cup finely chopped celery
1/2 cup peeled, seeded,
  finely chopped cucumber

1-1/2 tablespoons finely chopped dill or
  1-1/2 teaspoons dill weed
1 tablespoon lemon juice
1/2 teaspoon salt
Pinch of white pepper
Cucumber-Mint Sauce, page 152
Lettuce leaves
Lemon or lime wedges

Lightly oil a 3- to 4-cup decorative mold; set aside. Pour water into a small saucepan. Sprinkle gelatin over water; stir over low heat until gelatin is dissolved. Set aside until cool. In a medium bowl, combine mayonnaise and cooled gelatin mixture. Stir in fish, celery, cucumber, dill, lemon juice, salt and pepper. Pour mixture into oiled mold. Refrigerate 3 hours or until mousse is set. Prepare Cucumber-Mint Sauce; refrigerate. To serve, arrange lettuce leaves on a medium platter. Invert mold onto lettuce leaves; remove mold. Garnish with lemon or lime wedges. Serve sauce separately. Makes 6 to 8 servings.

Brunch Crab Soufflé

This do-ahead brunch dish is assembled the night before and baked before serving.

8 slices firm, white bread or
   cracked-wheat bread
3 tablespoons butter or margarine
2 (6-oz.) pkgs. frozen crabmeat, thawed,
   or 2 (6-oz.) cans crabmeat, drained
1/2 lb. mushrooms, sliced
1/4 cup sliced green onions

2 cups shredded Gruyère or
   Emmentaler cheese (8 oz.)
4 eggs
2-1/2 cups milk
1/2 teaspoon salt
1/2 teaspoon dry mustard
1/4 teaspoon pepper

Remove crusts from bread; reserve crusts. Cut trimmed bread into cubes; set aside. In a blender or food processor fitted with a metal blade, process crusts to make fine crumbs. Set aside 2 tablespoons crumbs. Reserve or freeze remaining crumbs for another purpose. Butter a 2-quart soufflé dish with 1 tablespoon butter or margarine. Dust with 2 tablespoons breadcrumbs. Flake crabmeat; remove cartilage. Melt remaining 2 tablespoons butter or margarine in a skillet. Add mushrooms; sauté until soft. Remove skillet from heat. Stir in green onions and crabmeat. In crumb-coated soufflé dish, alternate bread cubes, shredded cheese and crabmeat mixture. Make several layers, beginning and ending with bread cubes. In a large bowl, beat eggs; stir in milk, salt, mustard and pepper until blended. Slowly pour over layered ingredients in dish. Cover; refrigerate at least 4 hours before baking. Preheat oven to 325F (165C). Bake soufflé 1-1/2 hours or until top is golden brown and a knife inserted in center comes out clean. Makes 8 servings.

Shrimp-Gruyère Quiche

Serve with a fresh salad and a light dessert.

Pastry for 1 (10-inch) pie, unbaked
1/3 cup sliced green onions
1/4 lb. tiny shrimp or 1 (4-1/4-oz.) can
   tiny shrimp, drained
1-3/4 cups shredded Gruyère cheese (7 oz.)
4 eggs

1 cup half and half
1/2 teaspoon finely shredded lemon peel
2 tablespoons lemon juice
1/2 teaspoon salt
1/4 teaspoon ground nutmeg
1/4 teaspoon dry mustard

Preheat oven to 425F (220C). Roll out pastry to fit a 10-inch pie or tart pan. Place pastry in pan. Line pastry shell with foil; fill with rice, beans or metal pie weights. Bake 10 minutes; remove weights and foil from pastry shell. Reduce oven temperature to 325F (165C). Return pastry shell to oven; bake 10 minutes longer. Cool in pan on a wire rack. Combine green onions and shrimp. Sprinkle half the cheese into cooled pastry shell. Top with shrimp mixture. In a medium bowl, beat eggs; beat in half and half, lemon peel, lemon juice, salt, nutmeg and mustard. Pour over shrimp mixture; sprinkle with remaining cheese. Bake 55 to 65 minutes or until a knife inserted in center comes out clean. Cool 10 minutes before cutting. Serve warm or at room temperature. Makes 6 servings.

Sauces & Butters

Sauces are finishing touches that transform fish—regardless of the way it's cooked—into a superb meal. Lean, white, mild-flavor fish, such as sole, flounder, angler and whiting, are complemented by a delicate, rich sauce. Try Velouté Sauce, Beurre Blanc, Basic Hollandaise Sauce, Mayonnaise or any of the Hot Butter Sauces. Assertive-flavor fish, such as bluefish, mackerel, salmon and tuna, are compatible with a contrasting sauce. Try Vinaigrette Verte, Fresh Mexican Salsa and Seafood Cocktail Sauce.

One of the simplest classic French fish sauces is Velouté. Fish stock, clam juice or cooking liquid from poaching fish is enriched and thickened with butter and flour. Serve it with baked or broiled fish.

Two more sauces borrowed from the French are Basic Hollandaise Sauce and Mayonnaise. Mayonnaise is a cold sauce. It is used to make several other sauces, including Tartar Sauce and Sauce Rémoulade. My homemade Mayonnaise is a traditional recipe—and it's easy to make. Hollandaise Sauce is tricky to make, but if you use a blender or food processor, it's almost foolproof. The temperature must be hot enough to let the eggs *emulsify,* or be suspended in the mixture, but not cook. If they cook, the sauce will curdle.

Leave the egg out of Hollandaise Sauce and you'll have silky Beurre Blanc. The secret to making this sauce is to use chilled butter, keep the heat low, and whisk constantly. Set the Beurre Blanc aside until time to serve. Gently heat it in the top of a double boiler only until softened, but not melted.

Butter or margarine is the basis for an endless variety of sauces. Seasoned Butters, also called *compound butters,* are softened butter blended with savory seasonings. Spoon a dollop onto hot fish and watch it melt and run in rivulets, adding savory goodness. Or, shape the butter into a log and wrap in waxed paper. Store in the refrigerator and cut off pats as needed. Hot Butter Sauces—melted butter or margarine with herbs and other added flavorings—are easy and quick to prepare. Serve them with mild-flavor fish and shellfish.

Tartar Sauce   Photo on page 151.

A popular standby for all types of fish dishes.

1 cup Mayonnaise, page 144,
   or other mayonnaise
1/4 cup chopped cornichons or
   sour gherkin pickles

1 tablespoon drained capers
1 tablespoon finely chopped green onion
1 tablespoon finely chopped parsley

In a medium bowl, combine all ingredients; blend well. Makes about 1-1/4 cups.

Sauce Rémoulade

A delightful addition to cold poached fish and shellfish.

1 cup Mayonnaise, page 144,
   or other mayonnaise
1 garlic clove, minced
1 hard-cooked egg, finely chopped
1 tablespoon finely chopped parsley

2 teaspoons drained capers, chopped
1 teaspoon finely chopped tarragon or
   1/4 teaspoon dried leaf tarragon
1/2 teaspoon anchovy paste
1/2 teaspoon dry mustard

In a small bowl, combine all ingredients. Stir to blend. Cover and refrigerate at least 1 hour to let flavors blend. Makes about 1 cup.

Peppercorn-Mustard Sauce

Add zip to seafood dishes with this tasty combo.

1-1/4 to 1-1/2 teaspoons drained water-
   or brine-pack green peppercorns
1/4 cup Dijon-style mustard

1 cup Mayonnaise, page 144,
   or other mayonnaise
1 small garlic clove, minced

Crush 1 teaspoon green peppercorns; reserve remaining whole peppercorns. In a medium bowl, combine crushed peppercorns, mustard, mayonnaise and garlic. Fold in reserved whole peppercorns to taste. Makes 1-1/4 cups.

Creamy Dill Sauce

Dill is a classic herb used with seafood.

3/4 cup dairy sour cream
3/4 cup Mayonnaise, page 144,
   or other mayonnaise

1 tablespoon finely chopped green onion
2 teaspoons dill weed
1 teaspoon Beau Monde seasoning

In a medium bowl, combine all ingredients; blend well. Cover and refrigerate at least 15 minutes to let flavors blend. Makes 1-1/2 cups.

Mayonnaise

This easy-to-make mayonnaise is excellent in spreads and cold sauces.

2 egg yolks
1/4 teaspoon salt
Pinch of white pepper
1 tablespoon lemon juice,
   white-wine vinegar or
   tarragon vinegar

1 teaspoon Dijon-style mustard
1 cup vegetable oil or
   3/4 cup vegetable oil
   and 1/4 cup olive oil
1 tablespoon boiling water

Bring ingredients to room temperature before beginning. In a medium bowl, beat egg yolks with a whisk until pale, about 1 minute. Beat in salt, white pepper, lemon juice or vinegar and mustard. Begin adding oil, 1 drop at a time, beating vigorously and constantly. As mayonnaise begins to thicken, add remaining oil in a thin stream, beating constantly. After all oil has been incorporated, beat in water. Season to taste. Makes about 1-1/4 cups.

Blender Mayonnaise

If you like speed and ease of preparation, this is the mayonnaise for you!

1 egg
1 tablespoon lemon juice
1/4 teaspoon salt
Pinch of white pepper

1 cup vegetable oil or
   3/4 cup vegetable oil and
   1/4 cup olive oil
1 tablespoon boiling water

In a blender or food processor fitted with a metal blade, combine egg, lemon juice, salt and white pepper. Process 10 seconds. With motor running, add oil in a thin stream. Add water; process until blended. Season to taste. Makes 1 cup.

Pernod Mayonnaise

Anise-flavored liqueur, such as Pernod, is an excellent complement to seafood.

3 egg yolks
2 tablespoons red-wine vinegar
1 teaspoon Dijon-style mustard
1/2 teaspoon salt
1/8 teaspoon white pepper

1 cup vegetable oil
About 2 tablespoons Pernod or
   other anise-flavored liqueur
2 teaspoons finely chopped chives

In a blender or food processor fitted with a metal blade, process egg yolks, vinegar, mustard, salt and white pepper until well blended. With motor running, slowly add oil in a thin stream until mayonnaise is thick. Stir in liqueur and chives. Season to taste. Makes about 1-1/4 cups.

How to Make Mayonnaise

1/Add oil, one drop at a time, beating vigorously until slightly thickened.

2/Add remaining oil in a thin stream, beating constantly. Add water; season to taste.

Soy-Ginger Dip

For an Oriental touch, try this dipping sauce with batter-fried seafood.

1/4 cup soy sauce
1/4 cup water
1 to 2 tablespoons dry sherry
1 tablespoon sugar

1 tablespoon rice-wine vinegar or
   1-1/2 teaspoons white vinegar
1 teaspoon finely shredded gingerroot
1/8 teaspoon red (cayenne) pepper

In a small bowl, combine all ingredients; stir to blend. Makes about 2/3 cup.

Mustard-Dill Sauce

This excellent complement to salmon may be used with other hot or cold seafood.

2 tablespoons Dijon-style mustard
1 tablespoon white-wine vinegar
1-1/2 teaspoons sugar

1/4 cup chopped dill or
   1-1/2 teaspoons dill weed
1/2 cup light olive oil

In a blender or food processor fitted with a metal blade, combine mustard, vinegar, sugar and dill. Process several seconds to blend. With machine running, slowly add oil until mixture is blended and thickens slightly. Makes about 2/3 cup.

Beurre Blanc

One of the simplest-to-make but most exquisite sauces for fish.

1 tablespoon finely chopped shallot or
  white portion of green onion
2 tablespoons dry white wine
2 tablespoons white-wine vinegar

1 cup unsalted butter, chilled,
  cut into small cubes
Salt
White pepper

In a small saucepan, combine shallot or green onion, wine and vinegar. Cook until liquid reduces to about 1 tablespoon. Strain liquid into a medium saucepan. Discard shallot or green onion. Over low heat, whisk in butter, one piece at a time, until sauce is thick and creamy. Whisk constantly, removing from heat occasionally to prevent separation. Season with salt and white pepper to taste. If necessary, sauce can be held until serving by placing pan in a container of warm, *not simmering,* water. Makes about 1 cup.

Pineapple Beurre Blanc

Fruit juice gives this sauce a light, refreshing flavor—excellent with grilled seafood.

1/2 cup unsweetened pineapple juice
2 teaspoons finely chopped shallot or
  white portion of green onion
1-1/2 teaspoons lemon juice

8 to 10 tablespoons unsalted butter,
  chilled, cut into small cubes
Salt
White pepper

In a medium saucepan, combine pineapple juice, shallot or green onion and lemon juice. Cook until liquid reduces to 3 or 4 tablespoons. Reduce heat to low. Whisk in butter, one piece at a time, until sauce is thick and creamy. Whisk constantly, removing from heat occasionally to prevent separation. Season with salt and white pepper to taste. If necessary, sauce can be held until serving by placing pan in a container of warm, *not simmering,* water. Makes 1/2 to 2/3 cup.

Variation

Orange Beurre Blanc: Add 1/2 teaspoon finely shredded orange peel. Substitute 1/2 cup strained fresh orange juice for pineapple juice.

Leftover Beurre Blanc can be refrigerated. To use, bring back to room temperature; reheat in a double boiler, whisking constantly.

How to Make Beurre Blanc

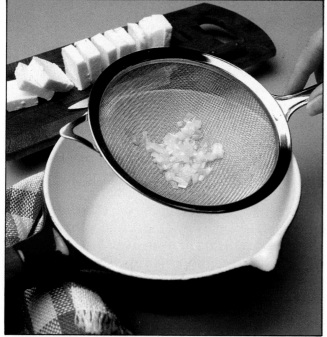

1/Cook shallot or green onion, wine and vinegar until liquid reduces to about 1 tablespoon. Strain liquid into a medium saucepan.

2/Whisk in butter, one piece at a time, until sauce is thick and creamy. Remove from heat occasionally to prevent separation.

Velouté Sauce

A classic French sauce to serve with baked or broiled fish.

1-1/2 tablespoons butter or margarine
1-1/2 tablespoons all-purpose flour
1 cup Fish Stock, page 101, or
    bottled clam juice

Salt
White pepper

Melt butter or margarine in a medium saucepan. Stir in flour. Cook over low heat 1 minute, stirring constantly. Gradually stir in Fish Stock or clam juice. Bring sauce to a boil; stirring constantly, boil until sauce thickens. Season with salt and white pepper to taste. Makes 1 cup.

Variation

To enrich sauce, stir in 3 to 4 tablespoons whipping cream after sauce comes to a boil. Do not boil after adding cream.

Mexican Salsa Verde

Fresh tomatillos and chilies are available in Mexican markets or large supermarkets.

2 fresh mild green Anaheim, poblano or
    pascilla chilies or
    canned mild green chilies
1 small fresh hot serrano or
    jalapeño chili or 1 teaspoon
    finely chopped canned
    hot green chilies or to taste
12 small tomatillos or
    1 (13-oz.) can tomatillos, undrained

Water
1/2 medium onion, chopped
1 garlic clove, minced
4 cilantro sprigs, if desired
1 tablespoon vegetable oil
1 cup chicken stock or broth
Salt and pepper

To handle fresh chilies, cover your hands with rubber or plastic gloves; after handling, do not touch your face or eyes. If using fresh chilies, roast over an open flame or in an oven broiler until skins are dark and blistered. Place in a paper or plastic food-storage bag; close top. Set aside 5 to 10 minutes. Peel blistered chilies. Under running water, skins remove easily. Cut in half; remove seeds and stem. If using fresh tomatillos, remove papery husks. Place in a medium saucepan. Add cold water to cover. Bring to a boil; reduce heat. Simmer 5 minutes; drain. Do not drain canned tomatillos. In a blender or food processor fitted with a metal blade, combine peeled fresh or canned chilies, cooked or canned tomatillos, onion, garlic and cilantro, if desired. Process until smooth. Heat oil in a heavy saucepan. Add chili mixture; cook over medium heat about 5 minutes, stirring constantly. Stir in stock or broth. Season with salt and pepper to taste. Partially cover; cook over low heat 20 minutes, stirring occasionally. Makes about 1-1/2 cups.

Fresh Mexican Salsa   Photo on page 151.

A colorful combination of raw ingredients with the piquant flavor of chilies.

1 fresh or canned serrano or jalapeño chili
1 large tomato, seeded, finely chopped
2 green onions, chopped
1/2 garlic clove, minced
2 teaspoons olive oil

1 to 2 teaspoons finely chopped cilantro
1/2 to 1 teaspoon lime juice
Salt
Freshly ground pepper

To handle fresh chili, cover your hands with rubber or plastic gloves; after handling, do not touch your face or eyes. Cut chili open lengthwise; remove seeds and pith from fresh or canned chili. Finely chop chili. In a small bowl, combine chopped chili, tomato, green onions, garlic, oil, cilantro and lime juice. Season with salt and pepper to taste. Taste and add more chilies, cilantro, lime juice, salt or pepper as needed. Makes about 3/4 cup.

How to Make Mexican Salsa Verde

1/Roast chilies over a flame or under broiler until skins are dark and blistered. Place in a paper or plastic storage bag 5 to 10 minutes.

2/Peel chilies under running water, if desired. Remove seeds and stems. Remove papery husks from fresh tomatillos.

Skordalia

Lightly toasting the nuts adds a special flavor to this Greek-inspired sauce.

**1/3 cup pine nuts or slivered almonds,
  lightly toasted**
1 egg
1 tablespoon lemon juice
1 tablespoon white-wine vinegar

1/2 teaspoon salt
Pinch of white pepper
3 garlic cloves
1/2 cup olive oil
1/2 cup vegetable oil

In a blender or food processor fitted with a metal blade, combine pine nuts or almonds, egg, lemon juice, vinegar, salt, white pepper and garlic. Process until garlic is finely chopped. Combine oils. With motor running, add oils in a thin stream; sauce will develop consistency of mayonnaise. Makes about 1-1/2 cups.

Toasting almonds or other nuts enhances the nutty flavor. Spread the nuts in a shallow pan; bake at 400F (205C) about 10 minutes, shaking or stirring the nuts occasionally. The darker the toasting, the more pronounced the flavor. Be careful not to get nuts so dark they become burned and bitter.

Italian Salsa Verde

This bright-green sauce has lots of assertive flavors.

1 cup tightly packed Italian flat-leaf
  parsley or other parsley sprigs
2 tablespoons finely chopped onion
3 or 4 canned flat anchovies, drained
1 large garlic clove
1/2 cup olive oil

1 to 1-1/2 tablespoons lemon juice
1-1/2 teaspoons finely chopped oregano or
  1/2 teaspoon dried leaf oregano
2-1/2 teaspoons finely chopped basil or
  3/4 teaspoon dried leaf basil
1/8 teaspoon pepper

In a blender or food processor fitted with a metal blade, combine all ingredients. Process until smooth and slightly thickened. Makes about 1 cup.

Watercress Sauce

A lovely cream sauce heightened with the color and flavor of watercress.

1 (2- to 3-oz.) bunch watercress
Water
1 cup whipping cream
1/2 cup dry white wine
About 1 tablespoon strained lemon juice

1/2 cup butter, preferably unsalted,
  chilled
White pepper
Salt, if desired

Rinse watercress; strip leaves from stems. Discard stems. Place leaves in a colander. Pour about 1 quart boiling water over leaves until wilted. Rinse under cold running water; pat dry with paper towels. In a blender or food processor fitted with a steel blade, puree leaves; set aside. In a medium saucepan, combine cream, wine and 1 tablespoon lemon juice. Stirring frequently, simmer over medium heat until reduced to 1/2 cup. Remove from heat. Cut cold butter into about 10 pieces. Whisk butter into cream mixture, one piece at a time. Butter must not melt but should develop into an emulsified sauce. Quickly whisk in watercress puree. Season with white pepper, lemon juice and salt, if desired. Serve immediately. Makes about 1 cup.

A good sauce can raise a plain fish dish from mediocrity to something special. Serve mild-flavor sauces with poached or steamed fish. Serve assertive or tangy sauces with fried, broiled or grilled fish that are strong flavored.

Clockwise from upper right: Orange-Soy Dipping Sauce from Fried Shrimp Balls, page 78; Italian Salsa Verde, above; Mustard Butter, page 156; Fresh Mexican Salsa, page 148; Tartar Sauce, page 143.

Mustard-Cream Sauce

A smooth yet tangy sauce that can be served hot or cold.

1/2 cup dry white wine
2 tablespoons finely chopped green onion,
   white portion only
1 cup whipping cream

3 to 4 teaspoons Dijon-style mustard
Salt
White pepper

In a medium saucepan, combine wine and green onion. Bring to a simmer; simmer 5 minutes or until liquid reduces to 2 tablespoons. Watch carefully, stirring occasionally, to prevent burning. Stir in cream; simmer 10 to 15 minutes or until sauce reduces to 3/4 cup. Whisk in mustard; season with salt and white pepper to taste. Serve hot or cold. To serve cold, cool to room temperature, then cover and refrigerate until chilled. Makes about 3/4 cup.

Cucumber-Mint Sauce

Serve this refreshing sauce with cold poached fish.

1/3 cup plain yogurt
2 tablespoons Mayonnaise, page 144,
   or other mayonnaise
1/4 cup peeled, seeded,
   finely chopped cucumber

2 teaspoons finely chopped mint or
   1/4 to 1/2 teaspoon crushed
   dried mint leaves
1/4 teaspoon minced garlic
1/4 teaspoon salt

In a medium bowl, combine all ingredients; blend well. Season to taste. Makes about 2/3 cup.

Tarragon-Mustard Sauce

Use as a sauce or dip for cold poached fish or chilled shrimp.

1 tablespoon Dijon-style mustard
1 tablespoon sugar
1 tablespoon white-wine vinegar
1 tablespoon finely chopped parsley

1-1/2 teaspoons finely chopped tarragon or
   1/4 to 1/2 teaspoon dried
   leaf tarragon
1/4 cup light olive oil or vegetable oil

In a small bowl, combine mustard, sugar, vinegar, parsley and tarragon; blend well. Add oil, beat until blended. Makes about 1/2 cup.

Vinaigrette Verte

A sauce for the true anchovy lover.

1-1/2 to 2 tablespoons red-wine vinegar
1 teaspoon finely shredded onion
6 canned flat anchovies, rinsed, drained
2 garlic cloves
2 tablespoons finely chopped parsley

1 tablespoon finely chopped basil or
 3/4 to 1 teaspoon dried leaf basil
Salt and pepper
6 tablespoons light olive oil

In a blender or food processor fitted with a metal blade, process vinegar, onion, anchovies, garlic, parsley, basil, salt and pepper until anchovies and garlic are finely chopped. Add oil; process until blended. Makes about 1/2 cup.

Seafood Cocktail Sauce

Serve this tangy sauce with chilled cooked shrimp, crabmeat or fried fish.

1/2 cup tomato-based chili sauce
1 tablespoon prepared horseradish
1 tablespoon lemon juice

2 teaspoons Worcestershire sauce
1/4 teaspoon salt
Pinch of red (cayenne) pepper

In a small bowl, combine all ingredients. Cover and refrigerate at least 2 hours to let flavors blend. Makes about 2/3 cup.

Shallot Sauce

A classic sauce served with oysters on-the-half-shell.

1/4 cup white wine
1/4 cup white-wine vinegar

1-1/2 tablespoons finely chopped shallots
1/4 to 1/2 teaspoon freshly ground pepper

In a small bowl, combine all ingredients. Makes about 1/2 cup.

The best fish for barbecuing are those that are rich in fat, such as mackerel and bluefish, or pronounced in flavor, such as swordfish, tuna and shark. Serve Mustard-Cream Sauce, opposite, as an accompaniment.

Basic Hollandaise Sauce

Hollandaise is a classic sauce with a light lemon flavor.

1 cup butter, preferably unsalted
3 egg yolks
1 tablespoon water

1 tablespoon freshly squeezed lemon juice
Pinch of salt
Pinch of white pepper

Melt butter in a small saucepan over low heat; keep warm. In top of a double boiler, beat egg yolks with water, lemon juice, salt and white pepper until pale, about 1 minute. Place over barely simmering water; whisk in warm butter, one drop at a time. When sauce begins to thicken, whisk in remaining butter in a thin stream, omitting milky residue at bottom of pan. If necessary, sauce can be held up to 1 hour by placing pan in a container of warm, *not simmering,* water. Season to taste. Makes about 1 cup.

Variation

Sauce Maltaise: Stir 1-1/2 to 2 teaspoons finely shredded orange peel and 1 to 2 tablespoons fresh orange juice into Basic Hollandaise Sauce.

Blender Hollandaise

Use a blender or food processor to make foolproof hollandaise sauce.

1 cup butter, preferably unsalted
3 egg yolks
Pinch of salt

Pinch of white pepper
1 tablespoon fresh lemon juice

Melt butter in a small saucepan over low heat; keep warm. In a blender or food processor fitted with a metal blade, process egg yolks, salt, white pepper and lemon juice until thoroughly blended. With motor running, add warm butter in a thin stream, omitting milky residue at bottom of pan. Season to taste. Makes about 1 cup.

Sauce Mousseline

A light sauce for delicate fish.

Basic or Blender Hollandaise Sauce, above, slightly cooled

1/3 cup whipping cream

Prepare Basic or Blender Hollandaise Sauce; cool. Just before serving, in a medium bowl, whip cream until soft peaks form. Fold whipped cream into cooled sauce. Makes about 1-1/2 cups.

Hot Butter Sauces

Melted butter or margarine, flavored with herbs and seasonings, is perfect with cooked fish or shellfish. Each makes about 1/2 cup.

Lemon-Garlic-Butter Sauce

1/2 cup butter or margarine
1 garlic clove, finely chopped
1 teaspoon finely shredded lemon peel
1-1/2 to 2 tablespoons lemon juice
1/2 teaspoon finely chopped chives or green-onion tops

Melt butter or margarine in a small saucepan; stir in remaining ingredients to taste.

Lime-Butter Sauce

1/2 cup butter or margarine
1 teaspoon finely shredded lime peel
1 tablespoon lime juice
1 to 2 teaspoons finely chopped cilantro or parsley

Melt butter or margarine in a small saucepan; stir in remaining ingredients to taste.

Nut-Butter Sauce

1/2 cup butter or margarine
2 tablespoons sliced or slivered almonds, or chopped pistachios, pecans, walnuts or hazelnuts

Melt butter or margarine in a small saucepan. Add nuts. Stirring occasionally, heat until butter or margarine bubbles and begins to brown and nuts are lightly toasted.

Mustard-Caper-Butter Sauce

1/2 cup butter or margarine
1 teaspoon dry mustard
1 tablespoon lemon juice
1/2 teaspoon capers
1 tablespoon finely chopped parsley

Melt butter or margarine in a small saucepan; stir in remaining ingredients to taste.

Dill-Butter Sauce

1/2 cup butter or margarine
2 to 3 teaspoons lemon juice
2 to 3 teaspoons finely chopped dill or 1 to 1-1/4 teaspoons dill weed

Melt butter or margarine in a small saucepan; stir in remaining ingredients to taste.

Tarragon-Butter Sauce

1/2 cup butter or margarine
1 tablespoon lemon juice
1-1/2 teaspoons chopped tarragon or 1/2 teaspoon dried leaf tarragon

Melt butter or margarine in a small saucepan over low heat; stir in remaining ingredients to taste.

Lime-Ginger-Butter Sauce

6 tablespoons butter or margarine
1 tablespoon fresh lime juice
1-1/2 to 2 teaspoons finely grated gingerroot

Melt butter or margarine in a small saucepan over low heat; stir in remaining ingredients to taste.

Seasoned Butters

Room-temperature butter or margarine, seasoned with herbs, is delicious with grilled, broiled or poached fish. Beat 1/2 cup butter or margarine until soft and light; beat in seasonings. Shape into a roll; wrap in waxed paper. Refrigerate until firm; slice to serve. Refrigerate up to 2 weeks or freeze up to 4 months. To freeze, wrap tightly in moisture-vapor-proof wrapping. Makes 1/2 cup.

Lemon-Parsley Butter

1/2 cup butter or margarine,
　room temperature
3 tablespoons finely chopped parsley
1/2 teaspoon finely chopped garlic
1 teaspoon finely shredded lemon peel
1 tablespoon lemon juice
1/4 teaspoon salt
Pinch of white pepper

Anchovy Butter

1/2 cup butter or margarine,
　room temperature
2 anchovy fillets, rinsed, drained
2 teaspoons lemon juice
2 teaspoons capers, chopped
1 garlic clove, minced

Lime-Cilantro Butter

1/2 cup butter or margarine,
　room temperature
1 to 2 tablespoons finely chopped cilantro
1/2 teaspoon finely shredded lime peel
4 teaspoons lime juice
1/4 teaspoon salt
Pinch of white pepper

Mustard Butter　Photo on page 151

1/2 cup butter or margarine,
　room temperature
1-1/2 tablespoons finely chopped parsley
2 teaspoons lemon juice
2-1/2 tablespoons Dijon-style mustard

Lime-Cumin Butter

1/2 cup butter or margarine,
　room temperature
1 teaspoon ground cumin
1/4 teaspoon finely shredded lime peel
1 tablespoon lime juice
1/4 teaspoon salt
1/8 to 1/4 teaspoon red (cayenne) pepper

Dill Butter

1/2 cup butter or margarine,
　room temperature
1 to 2 tablespoons finely chopped dill or
　1-1/2 teaspoons dill weed
1 teaspoon finely shredded lemon peel
2 teaspoons lemon juice
1/4 teaspoon salt
Pinch of white pepper

Pesto Butter

1/2 cup butter or margarine,
　room temperature
1-1/2 teaspoons finely chopped parsley
1-1/2 teaspoons dried leaf basil, crushed
2 teaspoons finely grated Parmesan cheese
1/2 garlic clove, finely chopped
1/8 teaspoon salt
Pinch of white pepper

Index

8.239381756